GACE 200 201 202

Basic Skills
Teacher Certification Exam

By: Sharon Wynne, M.S.
Southern Connecticut State University

"And, while there's no reason yet to panic, I think it's only prudent that we make preparations to panic."

XAMonline, INC.
Boston

XAMonline, Inc.
21 Orient Ave.
Melrose, MA 02176
Toll Free 1-800-509-4128
Email: info@xamonline.com
Web www.xamonline.com
Fax: 1-781-662-9268

Library of Congress Cataloging-in-Publication Data
Wynne, Sharon A.
   GACE: Basic Skills 200, 201, 202   Teacher Certification / Sharon A. Wynne.
   ISBN: 978-1-58197-257-3
   1. GACE: Basic Skills 200, 201, 202   2. Study Guides. 3. GACE
   4. Teachers' Certification & Licensure. 5. Careers

| Managing Editor | Dr. Harte Weiner | Senior Editor | |
| Production Coordinator | David Aronson | Copy Editor | Susan Andres |

Disclaimer:
The opinions expressed in this publication are the sole works of XAMonline and were created independently from the National Education Association (NEA), Educational Testing Service (ETS), or any State Department of Education, National Evaluation Systems (NES), or other testing affiliates.

Between the time of publication and printing, state specific standards as well as testing formats and website information may change that is not included in part or in whole within this product. Sample test questions are developed by XAMonline and they reflect similar content as on real tests; however, they are not former tests. XAMonline assembles content that aligns with state standards but makes no claims nor guarantees teacher candidates a passing score. Numerical scores are determined by testing companies such as NES or ETS and then are compared with individual state standards. A passing score varies from state to state.

Printed in the United States of America   œ-1
GACE: Basic Skills 200, 201, 202
ISBN: 978-1-58197-257-3

Table of Contents

Great Study and Testing Tips!

What to study in order to prepare for the subject assessments is the focus of this study guide but equally important is *how* you study.

You can increase your chances of truly mastering the information by taking some simple but effective steps.

Study Tips:

1. <u>Some foods aid the learning process</u>. Foods such as milk, nuts, seeds, rice, and oats help your study efforts by releasing natural memory enhancers called CCKs (*cholecystokinin*) composed of *tryptophan*, *choline*, and *phenylalanine*. All of these chemicals enhance the neurotransmitters associated with memory. Before studying, try a light, protein-rich meal of eggs, turkey, and fish. All of these foods release the memory-enhancing chemicals. The better the connections, the more you comprehend.

Likewise, before you take a test, stick to a light snack of energy boosting and relaxing foods. A glass of milk, a piece of fruit, or some peanuts all release various memory-boosting chemicals and help you to relax and focus on the subject at hand.

2. <u>Learn to take great notes</u>. A by-product of our modern culture is that we have grown accustomed to getting our information in short doses (i.e. TV news sound bites or *USA Today*-style newspaper articles.)

Consequently, we have subconsciously trained ourselves to assimilate information better in <u>neat little packages</u>. If your notes are scrawled all over the paper, it fragments the flow of the information. Strive for clarity. Newspapers use a standard format to achieve clarity. Your notes can be much clearer with proper formatting. A very effective format is called the *"Cornell Method."*

> Take a sheet of loose-leaf lined notebook paper and draw a line all the way down the paper about 1"–2" from the left-hand edge.
>
> Draw another line across the width of the paper about 1"–2" up from the bottom. Repeat this process on the reverse side of the page.

Look at the highly effective result. You have ample room for notes, a left-hand margin for special emphasis items or inserting supplementary data from the textbook, a large area at the bottom for a brief summary, and a little rectangular space for just about anything you want.

3. <u>Get the concept, then the details.</u> Too often, we focus on the details and do not gather an understanding of the concept. However, if you simply memorize only dates, places, or names, you may well miss the whole point of the subject.

A key way to understand things is to put them in your own words. If you are working from a textbook, automatically summarize each paragraph in your mind. If you are outlining text, do not simply copy the author's words.

Rephrase them in your own words. You remember your own thoughts and words much better than those of someone else and subconsciously tend to associate the important details with the core concepts.

4. <u>Ask Why?</u> Pull apart written material paragraph by paragraph and do not forget the captions under the illustrations.

Example: If the heading is "Stream Erosion," flip it around to read, "Why do streams erode?" Then answer the questions.

If you train your mind to think in a series of questions and answers, not only will you learn more, but you will also have less test anxiety because you are used to answering questions.

5. <u>Read for reinforcement and future needs.</u> Even if you only have ten minutes, put your notes or a book in your hand. Your mind is similar to a computer; you have to input data in order to have it processed. *By reading, you are creating the neural connections for future retrieval.* The more times you read something, the more you reinforce the learning of ideas.

Even if you do not fully understand something on the first pass, *your mind stores much of the material for later recall.*

6. <u>Relax to learn, so go into exile.</u> Our bodies respond to an inner clock called biorhythms. Burning the midnight oil works well for some people, but not everyone.

If possible, set aside a particular place to study that is free of distractions. Shut off the television, cell phone, and pager and exile your friends and family during your study period.

If silence really bothers you, try background music. Light classical music at a low volume has been shown to aid in concentration over other types. Music without lyrics that evokes pleasant emotions is highly suggested. Try just about anything by Mozart. It relaxes you.

7. Use arrows, not highlighters. At best, it is difficult to read a page full of yellow, pink, blue, and green streaks. Try staring at a neon sign for a while and you will soon see that the horde of colors obscure the message.

A quick note, a brief dash of color, an underline, or an arrow pointing to a particular passage is much clearer than a horde of highlighted words.

8. Budget your study time. Although you should not ignore any of the material, *allocate your available study time in the same ratio that topics may appear on the test.*

Testing Tips:

1. Get smart, play dumb. Do not read anything into the question. Do not assume that the test writer is looking for something else than what is asked. Stick to the question as written and do not read extra things into it.

2. Read the question and all the choices *twice* before answering the question. You may miss something by not carefully reading and then re-reading both the question and the answers.

If you really do not have a clue as to the right answer, leave it blank on the first time through. Go on to the other questions, as they may provide a clue as to how to answer the skipped questions.

If later on, you still cannot answer the skipped ones . . . ***guess.*** The only penalty for guessing is that you *might* get it wrong. Only one thing is certain; if you do not put anything down, you will get it wrong!

3. Turn the question into a statement. Look at the way the questions are worded. The syntax of the question usually provides a clue. Does it seem more familiar as a statement rather than as a question? Does it sound strange?

By turning a question into a statement, you may be able to spot if an answer sounds right, and it may trigger memories of material you have read.

4. Look for hidden clues. It is actually very difficult to compose multiple-foil (choice) questions without giving away part of the answer in the options presented.

In most multiple-choice questions, you can often readily eliminate one or two of the potential answers. This leaves you with only two real possibilities and automatically your odds go to fifty-fifty for very little work.

5. Trust your instincts. For every fact that you have read, you subconsciously retain something of that knowledge. On questions about which you are not really certain, go with your basic instincts. **Your first impression on how to answer a question is usually correct.**

6. Mark your answers directly on the test booklet. Do not bother trying to fill in the optical scan sheet on the first pass through the test.

Be careful not to mismark your answers when you transcribe them to the scan sheet.

7. Watch the clock! You have a set amount of time to answer the questions. Do not get bogged down trying to answer a single question at the expense of ten questions you can more readily answer.

COMPETENCY 1.0   UNDERSTAND THE MAIN IDEA AND SUPPORTING DETAILS IN WRITTEN MATERIAL

Skill 1.1   Identify the explicit and implicit main idea of a paragraph or passage

The main idea of a passage or paragraph is the basic message, idea, point concept, or meaning that the author wants to convey to you, the reader. Understanding the main idea of a passage or paragraph is the key to understanding the more subtle components of the author's message. The main idea is what is being said about a topic or subject. Once you have identified the basic message, you will have an easier time answering other questions that test critical skills.

Main ideas are either *stated* or *implied.* A *stated main idea* is explicit—it is directly expressed in a sentence or two in the paragraph or passage. An *implied main idea* is suggested by the overall reading selection. In the first case, you need not pull information from various points in the paragraph or passage in order to form the main idea because the author already states it. If a main idea is implied, however, you must formulate, in your own words, a main idea statement by condensing the overall message contained in the material itself.

Skill 1.2   **Identify the statement or statements that best express the main idea of a paragraph or passage**

Practice Question: Read the following passage and select an answer

Sometimes too much of a good thing can become a very bad thing indeed. In an earnest attempt to consume a healthy diet, dietary supplement enthusiasts have been known to overdose. Vitamin C, for example, long thought to help people ward off cold viruses, is currently being studied for its possible role in warding off cancer and other diseases that cause tissue degeneration. Unfortunately, an overdose of vitamin C—more than 10,000 mg—on a daily basis can cause nausea and diarrhea. Calcium supplements, commonly taken by women, are helpful in warding off osteoporosis. More than just a few grams a day, however, can lead to stomach upset and even kidney and bladder stones. Niacin, proven useful in reducing cholesterol levels, can be dangerous in large doses to those who suffer from heart problems, asthma, or ulcers.

The main idea expressed in this paragraph is:

      A.   supplements taken in excess can be a bad thing indeed
      B.   dietary supplement enthusiasts have been known to overdose
      C.   vitamins can cause nausea, diarrhea, and kidney or bladder stones
      D.   people who take supplements are preoccupied with their health

Answer: Answer A is a paraphrase of the first sentence and provides a general framework for the rest of the paragraph—excess supplement intake is bad. The rest of the paragraph discusses the consequences of taking too many vitamins. Options B and C refer to major details and Option D introduces the idea of preoccupation, which is not included in this paragraph.

Skill 1.3 Recognize ideas that support, illustrate, or elaborate on the main idea of a paragraph or passage

Supporting details are examples, facts, ideas, illustrations, cases, and anecdotes used by a writer to explain, expand upon, and develop the more general main idea. A writer's choice of supporting materials is determined by the nature of the topic being covered. Supporting details are specifics that relate directly to the main idea. Writers select and shape material according to their purposes. An advertisement writer seeking to persuade the reader to buy a particular running shoe, for instance, will emphasize only the positive characteristics of the shoe for advertisement copy. A columnist for a running magazine, on the other hand, might list the good and bad points about the same shoe in an article recommending appropriate shoes for different kind of runners. Both major details (those that directly support the main idea), and minor details (those that provide interesting, but not always essential, information) help create a well-written and fluid passage.

In the following paragraph, the sentences in **bold print** provide a skeleton of a paragraph on the benefits of recycling. The sentences in bold are generalizations, which by themselves, do not explain the need to recycle. The sentences in *italics* add details to SHOW the general points in bold. Notice how the supporting details help you understand the necessity for recycling.

While one day recycling may become mandatory in all states, right now it is voluntary in many communities. *Those of us who participate in recycling are amazed by how much material is recycled.* **For many communities, the blue-box recycling program has had an immediate effect.** *By just recycling glass, aluminum cans, and plastic bottles, we have reduced the volume of disposable trash by one-third, thus extending the useful life of local landfills by over a decade. Imagine the difference if those dramatic results were achieved nationwide.* **The amount of reusable items we thoughtlessly dispose of is staggering.** *For example, Americans dispose of enough steel everyday to supply Detroit car manufacturers for three months. Additionally, we dispose of enough aluminum annually to rebuild the nation's air fleet. These statistics, available from the Environmental Protection Agency (EPA), should encourage all of us to watch what we throw away.* **Clearly, recycling in our homes and in our communities directly improves the environment.**

Notice how the author's supporting examples enhance the message of the paragraph and relate to the author's thesis noted above. If you only read the boldface sentences, you have a glimpse at the topic. This paragraph of illustration, however, is developed through numerous details creating specific images: *reduced the volume of disposable trash by one-third, extended the useful life of local landfills by over a decade, enough steel everyday to supply Detroit car manufacturers for three months, enough aluminum to rebuild the nation's air fleet.* If the writer had merely written a few general sentences, as those shown in boldface, you would not fully understand the vast amount of trash involved in recycling or the positive results of current recycling efforts.

COMPETENCY 2.0   INDENTIFY A WRITER'S PURPOSE AND POINT OF VIEW

Skill 2.1   Recognize a writer's expressed or implied purpose for writing

An essay is an extended discussion of a writer's point of view about a particular topic. This point of view may be supported by using such writing modes as examples, argument and persuasion, and analysis or comparison/contrast. In any case, a good essay is clear, coherent, well organized, and fully developed.

When an author sets out to write a passage, he/she usually has a purpose for doing so. That purpose may be simply to give information that might be interesting or useful to some reader or other. It may be to persuade the reader to a point of view or to move the reader to act in a particular way; it may be to tell a story; or it may be to describe something in such a way that an experience becomes available to the reader through one of the five senses. Following are the primary devices for expressing a particular purpose in a piece of writing:

- **Basic expository writing** simply gives information not previously known about a topic or is used to explain or define one. Facts, examples, statistics, cause and effect, direct tone, objective rather than subjective delivery, and non-emotional information are presented in a formal manner.

- **Descriptive writing** centers on person, place, or object, using concrete and sensory words to create a mood or impression and arranging details in a chronological or spatial sequence.

- **Narrative writing** is developed using an incident or anecdote or related series of events. Chronology, the five W's, topic sentence, and conclusion are essential ingredients.

- **Persuasive writing** implies the writer's ability to select vocabulary and arrange facts and opinions in such a way as to direct the actions of the listener/reader. Persuasive writing may incorporate exposition and narration as they illustrate the main idea.

- **Journalistic writing** is theoretically free of author bias. It is essential when relaying information about an event, person, or thing that it be factual and objective. Provide students with an opportunity to examine newspapers and create their own. Many newspapers have educational programs that are offered free to schools.

Skill 2.2   **Evaluate the appropriateness of written material for a specific purpose or audience**

See Skill 2.1.

Skill 2.3 **Recognize the likely effect on an audience of a writer's language choices using the content, word choice, and phrasing of a passage to determine a writer's purpose or point of view**

Tailoring language for a particular **audience** is an important skill. Writing to be read by a business associate will surely sound different from writing to be read by a younger sibling. Not only are the vocabularies different, but the formality/informality of the discourse will need to be adjusted.

The things to be aware of in determining what the language should be for a particular audience, then, hinge on two things: **word choice** and **formality/informality**. The most formal language does not use contractions or slang. The most informal language will probably feature a more casual use of common sayings and anecdotes. Formal language will use longer sentences and will not sound like a conversation. The most informal language will use shorter sentences—not necessarily simple sentences—but shorter constructions and may sound like a conversation.

In both formal and informal writing, there exists a **tone**, the writer's attitude toward the material and/or readers. Tone may be playful, formal, intimate, angry, serious, ironic, outraged, baffled, tender, serene, or depressed, etc. Both the subject matter and the audience dictate the overall tone of a piece of writing. Tone is also related to the actual words that make up the document, as we attach affective meanings, called **connotations,** to words. Gaining this conscious control over language makes it possible to use language appropriately in various situations and to evaluate its uses in literature and other forms of communication. By evoking the proper responses from readers/listeners, we can prompt them to take action. The following questions are an excellent way to assess the audience and tone of a given piece of writing.

1. Who is your audience? (friend, teacher, business person, or someone else)
2. How much does this person know about you and/or your topic?
3. What is your purpose? (to prove an argument, to persuade, to amuse, to register a complaint, to ask for a raise, etc)
4. What emotions do you have about the topic? (nervous, happy, confident, angry, sad, no feelings at all)
5. What emotions do you want to register with your audience? (anger, nervousness, happiness, boredom, interest)
6. What persona do you need to create in order to achieve your purpose?
7. What choice of language is best suited to achieving your purpose with your particular subject? (slang, friendly but respectful, formal)
8. What emotional quality do you want to transmit to achieve your purpose (matter of fact, informative, authoritative, inquisitive, sympathetic, or angry) and to what degree do you want to express this tone?

Skill 2.4 Recognize how intended audience and purpose affect an author's choice of style and content

The **tone** of a written passage is the author's attitude toward the subject matter. The tone (mood, feeling) is revealed through the qualities of the writing itself and is a direct product of such stylistic elements as language and sentence structure. The tone of the written passage is much like a speaker's voice; instead of being spoken, however, it is the product of words on a page.

Often, writers have an emotional stake in the subject, and their purpose, either explicitly or implicitly, is to convey those feelings to the reader. In such cases, the writing is generally subjective, that is, it stems from opinions, judgments, values, ideas, and feelings. Both sentence structure (syntax) and word choice (diction) are instrumental tools in creating tone.

Tone may be thought of generally as positive, negative, or neutral. Below is a statement about snakes that demonstrates this.

> *Many species of snakes live in Florida. Some of those species, both poisonous and non-poisonous, have habitats that coincide with those of human residents of the state.*

The voice of the writer in this statement is neutral. The sentences are declarative (not exclamations or fragments or questions). The adjectives are few and nondescript—*many, some, poisonous* (balanced with *non-poisonous*). Nothing much in this brief paragraph would alert the reader to the feelings of the writer about snakes. The paragraph has a neutral, objective, detached, impartial tone.

Then again, if the writer's attitude toward snakes involves admiration or even affection, the tone would generally be positive.

> *Florida's snakes are a tenacious bunch. When they find their habitats invaded by humans, they cling to their home territories as long as they can, as if vainly attempting to fight off the onslaught of the human hordes.*

An additional message emerges in this paragraph—the writer quite clearly favors snakes over people. The writer uses adjectives such as *tenacious* to describe his/her feelings about snakes. The writer also humanizes the reptiles, making them brave, beleaguered creatures. Obviously, the writer is more sympathetic to snakes than to people in this paragraph.

If the writer's attitude toward snakes involves active dislike and fear, then the tone would also reflect that attitude by being negative.

Countless species of snakes, some more dangerous than others, still lurk on the urban fringes of Florida's towns and cities. They will often invade domestic spaces, terrorizing people and their pets.

Here, obviously, the snakes are the villains. They *lurk,* they *invade,* and they *terrorize.* The tone of this paragraph might be said to be distressed about snakes.

In the same manner, a writer can use language to portray characters as good or bad. A writer uses positive and negative adjectives, as seen above, to convey the manner of a character.

COMPETENCY 3.0   ANALYZE THE RELATIONSHIP AMONG IDEAS IN WRITTEN MATERIAL

Skill 3.1   Identify sequence of events or steps

The ability to organize events or steps provided in a passage (especially when presented in random order) serves a useful purpose, and it encourages the development of logical thinking and the processes of analysis and evaluation.

Working through and discussing with your students examples such as the one below help students to gain valuable practice in sequencing events.

The relationship between sentences is the link that conceptually ties one sentence to another. The relationship may be explicit, in which case a transition or clue word helps identify the connection. The relation may be implicit, in which case you must closely examine the elements found in each sentence and often in the material between the sentences.

Practice Question: identify the proper order of events or steps.

1. Matt had tied a knot in his shoelace.
2. Matt put on his green socks because they were clean and complemented the brown slacks he was wearing.
3. Matt took a bath and trimmed his toenails.
4. Matt put on his brown slacks.

Answer: The proper order of events is 3, 4, 2, and 1.

Skill 3.2   Identify types of relationships (e.g., cause and effect, analogies, classification)

Most sentences cannot meaningfully stand alone. To read a passage without recognizing how each sentence is linked to those around it is to lose the passage's meaning. There are many ways in which sentences can be connected to one another.

Addition – One sentence is "tacked on" to another, without making one sentence depend upon the other. Both are equally important.

> *Joanna recently purchased a new stereo system, computer, and home alarm system. She **also** put down a payment on a new automobile.*

Clarification – One sentence restates the point of an earlier one, but in different terms.

> *The national debt is growing continually. **In fact**, by next year, it may be five trillion dollars.*

Comparison/Contrast – Connection is one of similarity or difference.

> *Shelley's strained relationship with his father led the poet to a life of rebellion. **Likewise**, Byron's Bohemian lifestyle may be traced to his ambivalence towards authority.*

Example – One sentence works to make another more concrete or specific.

> *Sarah has always been an optimistic person. She believes that when she graduates from college she will get the job of her choice. (implicit)*

Location/Spatial Order – The relationship between sentences shows the placement of objects or items relative to each other in space.

> *The park was darkened by the school building's shadow. However, the sun still splashed the front window with light. (implicit)*

Cause/Effect – One event (cause) brings about the second event (effect).

> *General Hooker failed to anticipate General Lee's bold maneuver. **As a result**, Hooker's army was nearly routed by a smaller force.*

Summary – A summary sentence surveys and captures the most important points of the previous sentence(s).

Every Fourth of July, Ralph brings his whole family to the local parade; every Memorial Day, he displays the flag; and every November 4, he votes. **On the whole**, *he's a patriotic American.*

Skill 3.3 Analyze relationships between or among similar ideas or ideas in opposition

Whenever there are two ideas in opposition, there is the ghost of an "either ... or" conceptual basis lurking invisibly in the background of the "pro/con" setting.

For example, one person may argue that automobiles are a safer mode of transportation than are motorcycles and support that contention with statistics showing that fatalities are more frequent per accident in motorcycle crashes than in car crashes.

The opposition to this argument may counter that while fatalities are more frequent per accident in motorcycle accidents, it is erroneous to overgeneralize from that statistic that motorcycles are "therefore more dangerous."

Thus, each participant in the argument has assumed a position of "either ... or," that is to say, the automobile is "either" safer than the motorcycle, or it is not (or the motorcycle is "either" safer than the automobile or it is not). With the argument thus formulated, a conclusion acceptable to both sides is not likely to happen.

Here is a short essay showing how to avoid this deadlock.

Which is safer? The car or the motorcycle?

Most experienced drivers would agree that while it is more exhilarating to ride a motorcycle than to drive an automobile, it is illogical to therefore conclude that this exhilaration leads to careless driving and, therefore, more accidents, deaths, and injuries to motorcycle riders than car drivers. The critical concept to be understood here is not exhilaration, which is a given, but how the exhilaration comes about and is a cause of serious injury and death of motorcycle riders.

There is safe and unsafe thrill seeking. Exhilaration is defined as the "state of being stimulated, refreshed, or elated." An example of safe exhilaration is the excitement of sledding downhill, which results in the sled rider feeling stimulated, refreshed, and/or elated.

Unsafe exhilaration, which is usually the consequence of reckless thrill seeking, is therefore a state of being over-stimulated, frightened, and depressed by terror.

Which then causes exhilaration that is more dangerous, the car or the motorcycle? The answer is that the two forms of exhilaration are the consequence not of the motorcycle or the automobile, per se, but of the operation of the respective vehicles. Without an operator, both vehicles are metal entities, sitting in space, neither threatening nor harmful to anyone.

Therefore, neither the motorcycle nor the car is more or less dangerous than one another is. It is the attitude of their operators that creates the danger, death, and dismemberment resultant from accidents.

Notice how the writer has avoided the logical trap of the "either ... or" construction built into the "pro con" argument by defining the key term *exhilaration* to clarify the issue (and shift the focus to the operator). The writer also resolves the either ... or dilemma BY arguing the operators of the vehicles are responsible for negative consequences, not the vehicles themselves.

Skill 3.4   Predict outcomes

An **inference** is sometimes called an *educated guess* because it requires that you go beyond the strictly obvious to create additional meaning by taking the text one logical step further. Inferences and conclusions are based on the content of the passage—that is, on what the passage says or how the writer says it—and are derived by reasoning.

Inference is an essential and automatic component of most reading. For example, in making educated guesses about the meaning of unknown words, about the author's main idea, or about whether he or she is writing with a bias. Such is the essence of inference. You use your own ability to reason in order to figure out what the writer implies. As a reader, then, you must often logically extend meaning that is only implied.

Consider the following example. Assume you are an employer, and you are reading over the letters of reference submitted by a prospective employee for the position of clerk/typist in your real estate office. The position requires the applicant to be neat, careful, trustworthy, and punctual. You come across this letter of reference submitted by an applicant:

To whom it may concern,

Todd Finley has asked me to write a letter of reference for him. I am well qualified to do so because he worked for me for three months last year. His duties included answering the phone, greeting the public, and producing some simple memos and notices on the computer. Although Todd initially had few computer skills and little knowledge of telephone etiquette, he did acquire some during his stay with us. Todd's manner of speaking, both on the telephone and with the clients who came to my establishment, could be described as casual. He was particularly effective when communicating with peers. Please contact me by telephone if you wish to have further information about my experience.

Here the writer implies, rather than openly states, the main idea. This letter calls attention to itself because there is a problem with its tone. A truly positive letter would say something such as "I have the distinct honor to recommend Todd Finley." Here, however, the letter simply verifies that Todd worked in the office. Second, the praise is obviously lukewarm. For example, the writer says that Todd "was particularly effective when communicating with peers." An educated guess translates that statement into a nice way of saying Todd was not serious about his communication with clients.

Skill 3.5   Draw conclusions inductively and deductively from information stated or implied in a passage.

In order to draw **inferences** and make **conclusions**, a reader must use prior knowledge and apply it to the current situation. A conclusion or inference is never stated. You must rely on your common sense.

Practice Questions: Read the following passages and select an answer

1.   Tim Sullivan had just turned fifteen. As a birthday present, his parents had given him a guitar and a certificate for ten guitar lessons. He had always shown a love of music and a desire to learn an instrument. Tim began his lessons and before long, he was making up his own songs. At the music studio, Tim met Josh, who played the piano, and Roger, whose instrument was the saxophone. They all shared the same dream—to start a band— and each was praised by his teacher as having real talent.

From this passage, one can infer that

A. Tim, Roger, and Josh are going to start their own band.
B. Tim is going to give up his guitar lessons.
C. Tim, Josh, and Roger will no longer be friends.
D. Josh and Roger are going to start their own band.

2.   The Smith family waited patiently around carousel number 7 for their luggage to arrive. They were exhausted after their five-hour trip and were anxious to get to their hotel. After about an hour, they realized that they no longer recognized any of the other passengers' faces. Mrs. Smith asked the person who appeared to be in charge if they were at the right carousel. The man replied, "Yes, this is it, but we finished unloading that baggage almost half an hour ago."

From the man's response, we can infer that

A. The Smiths were ready to go to their hotel.
B. The Smiths' luggage was lost.
C. The man had their luggage.
D. They were at the wrong carousel.

Answers:

1. (A) is the correct choice. Given the facts that Tim wanted to be a musician and start his own band, after meeting others who shared the same dreams, we can infer that they joined in an attempt to make their dreams become a reality.

2. Since the Smiths were still waiting for their luggage, we know that they were not yet ready to go to their hotel. From the man's response, we know that they were not at the wrong carousel and that he did not have their luggage. Therefore, though not directly stated, it appears that their luggage was lost. Choice (B) is the correct answer.

COMPETENCY 4.0   USE CRITICAL REASONING SKILLS TO EVALUATE WRITTEN MATERIAL

Skill 4.1   Evaluate the stated or implied assumptions upon which the validity of a writer's argument depends

On the test, the terms **valid** and **invalid** have special meaning. If an argument is valid, it is reasonable. It is objective (not biased) and can be supported by evidence. If an argument is invalid, it is not reasonable. It is not objective. In other words, one can find evidence of bias.

Practice Questions: Read the following passages and select an answer.

1.   Most dentists agree that Bright Smile Toothpaste is the best for fighting cavities. It tastes good and leaves your mouth minty fresh.

Is this a valid or invalid argument?

(A) valid
(B) invalid

2.   It is difficult to decide who will make the best presidential candidate, Senator Johnson or Senator Keeley. They have both been involved in scandals and have both gone through messy divorces while in office.

Is this argument valid or invalid?

(A) valid
(B) invalid

Answers:

(A) is the correct choice. The author appears to be listing facts. He does not seem to favor one candidate over the other.

It is invalid (B). It mentions that *most* dentists agree. What about those who do not agree? The author is clearly exhibiting bias in leaving those who disagree out.

Skill 4.2   Judging the relevance or importance of facts, examples, or graphic data to a writer's argument

It is important to assess whether or not a sentence contributes to the overall task of supporting the main idea continually. When a sentence is deemed irrelevant, it is best either to omit it from the passage or to make it relevant by one of the following strategies:

1. Adding detail—Sometimes a sentence can seem out of place if it does not contain enough information to link it to the topic. Adding specific information can show how the sentence is related to the main idea.

2. Adding an example—This is especially important in passages in which information is being argued, compared, or contrasted. Examples can support the main idea and give the document overall credibility.

3. Using diction effectively—It is important to understand connotation, avoid ambiguity, and avoid too much repetition when selecting words.

4. Adding transitions—Transitions are extremely helpful for making sentences relevant because they are specifically designed to connect one idea to another. They can also reduce a paragraph's choppiness.

Skill 4.3   Evaluate the logic of a writer's argument and the validity of analogies

An argument is a generalization that is proven or supported with facts. If the facts are not accurate, the generalization remains unproven. Using inaccurate *facts* to support an argument is called a *fallacy* in reasoning. Some factors to consider in judging whether the facts used to support an argument are accurate are as follows:

1. Are the facts current or are they out-of-date? For example, if the proposition is "birth defects in babies born to drug-using mothers are increasing," then the data must include the latest available.
2. Another important factor to consider in judging the accuracy of a fact is its source. Where was the data obtained and is that source reliable?
3. The calculations on which the facts are based may be unreliable. It is a good idea to run one's own calculations before using a piece of derived information.

Even facts that are true and have a sharp impact on the argument may not be relevant to the case at hand.

1. Health statistics from an entire state may have no relevance, or little relevance, to a particular county or zip code. Statistics from an entire country cannot be used to prove very much about a particular state or county.
2. An analogy can be useful in making a point, but the comparison must match up in all characteristics or it will not be relevant. Analogy should be used very carefully. It is often just as likely to destroy an argument, as it is to strengthen it.

The importance or significance of a fact may not be sufficient to strengthen an argument. For example, of the millions of immigrants in the U.S., using a single family to support a solution to the immigration problem will not make much difference overall even though those single-example arguments are often used to support one approach or another. They may achieve a positive reaction, but they will not prove that one solution is better than another is. If enough cases were cited from a variety of geographical locations, the information might be significant.

How much is enough? Three strong supporting facts are sufficient to establish the thesis of an argument. For example:

Conclusion: All green apples are sour.

- When I was a child, I bit into a green apple from my grandfather's orchard, and it was sour.

- I once bought green apples from a roadside vendor, and when I bit into one, it was sour.
- My grocery store had a sale on green Granny Smith apples last week, and I bought several only to find that they were sour when I bit into one.

The fallacy in the above argument is that the sample was insufficient. A more exhaustive search of literature, etc., will probably turn up some green apples that are not sour.

Sometimes more than three arguments are too many. On the other hand, it is not unusual to hear public speakers, particularly politicians, who will cite a long litany of facts to support their positions.

A very good example of the omission of facts in an argument is the résumé of an applicant for a job. The applicant is arguing that he/she should be chosen to be awarded a particular job. The application form will ask for information about past employment, and unfavorable dismissals from jobs in the past may just be omitted. Employers are usually suspicious of periods of time when the applicant has not listed an employer.

A writer makes choices about which facts will be used and which will be discarded in developing an argument. Those choices may exclude anything that is not supportive of the point of view the arguer is taking. It is always a good idea for the reader to do some research to spot the omissions and to ask whether they have impact on acceptance of the point of view presented in the argument.

No judgment is either black or white. If the argument seems too neat or too compelling, there are probably facts that might be relevant that have not been included.

Skill 4.4   Distinguish between fact and opinion

Facts are verifiable statements. Opinions are statements that must be supported in order to be accepted, such as beliefs, values, judgments, or feelings. Facts are objective statements used to support subjective opinions. For example, "Jane is a bad girl" is an opinion. However, "Jane hit her sister with a baseball bat" is a *fact* upon which the opinion is based. Judgments are opinions—decisions or declarations based on observation or reasoning that express approval or disapproval. Facts report what has happened or exists and come from observation, measurement, or calculation. Facts can be tested and verified whereas opinions and judgments cannot. They can only be supported with facts.

Most statements cannot be so clearly distinguished. "I believe that Jane is a bad girl" is a fact. The speaker knows what he/she believes. However, it obviously includes a judgment that could be disputed by another person who might believe otherwise. Judgments are not usually so firm. They are, rather, plausible opinions that provoke thought or lead to factual development.

Mickey Mantle replaced Joe DiMaggio, a Yankees' center fielder, in 1952.

This is a fact. If necessary, evidence can be produced to support this.

First year players are more ambitious than seasoned players are.

This is an opinion. There is no proof to support that everyone feels this way

Practice Questions: Decide if the statement is fact or opinion.

1. The Inca were a group of Indians who ruled an empire in South America.

    (A) fact
    (B) opinion

2. The Inca were clever.

    (A) fact
    (B) opinion

3. The Inca built very complex systems of bridges.

    (A) fact
    (B) opinion

Answers:
1. (A) is the correct answer. Research can prove this true.
2. (B) is the correct answer. It is doubtful that all people who have studied the Inca agree with this statement. Therefore, no proof is available.
3. (A) is the correct answer. As it can with question number one, research can prove this true.

Skill 4.5 Assess the credibility or objectivity of a writer or source of written material

Bias is defined as an opinion, feeling, or influence that strongly favors one side in an argument. A statement or passage is biased if an author attempts to convince a reader of something.

Is there evidence of bias in the following statement?

> *Using a calculator cannot help a student understand the process of graphing, so its use is a waste of time.*

Since the author makes it perfectly clear that he does not favor the use of the calculator in graphing problems, the answer is yes, there is evidence of bias. He has included his opinion in this statement.

Practice Question: Read the following paragraph and select an answer

There are teachers who feel that computer programs are quite helpful in helping students grasp certain math concepts. There are also those who disagree with this feeling. It is up to each individual math teacher to decide if computer programs benefit her particular group of students.

Is there evidence of bias in this paragraph?
(A) yes
(B) no

Answer: Since the author makes it perfectly clear that he does not favor the use of the calculator in graphing problems, the answer is (A). He has included his opinion in this statement.

*   *   *

"The sky is blue." "The sky looks like rain." One is a fact and the other an opinion.

This is because one is **readily provable by objective empirical data**, while the other is a **subjective evaluation based upon personal bias**. This means that facts are things that can be proved by the usual means of study and experimentation. We can look and see the color of the sky. Since the shade we are observing is expressed as the color blue and is an accepted norm, the observation that the sky is blue is therefore a fact. (Of course, this depends on other external factors such as time and weather conditions.)

This brings us to our next idea—that it looks like rain. This is a subjective observation in that an individual's perception will differ from that of another. What looks like rain to one person will not necessarily look like that to another person. The question thus remains as to how to differentiate fact from opinion. The best and only way is to ask oneself if what is being stated can be proved from other sources, by other methods, or by the simple process of **reasoning**.

Primary and secondary sources

The resources used to support a piece of writing can be divided into two major groups: primary sources and secondary sources.

Primary sources are works, records, etc. that were created during the period being studied or immediately after it. Secondary sources are works written significantly after the period being studied and based upon primary sources. Primary sources are the basic materials that provide raw data and information. Secondary sources are the works that contain the explications of, and judgments on, this primary material.

Primary sources include the following kinds of materials:

- Documents that reflect the immediate, everyday concerns of people: memoranda, bills, deeds, charters, newspaper reports, pamphlets, graffiti, popular writings, journals or diaries, records of decision-making bodies, letters, receipts, snapshots, etc.
- Theoretical writings that reflect care and consideration in composition and an attempt to convince or persuade. The topic will generally be deeper and reflect more pervasive values than is the case with *immediate* documents. These may include newspaper or magazine editorials, sermons, political speeches, philosophical writings, etc.
- Narrative accounts of events, ideas, trends, etc. written with intentionality by someone contemporary with the events described.
- Statistical data, although statistics may be misleading
- Literature and nonverbal materials, novels, stories, poetry, and essays from the period, as well as coins, archaeological artifacts, and art produced during the period

Secondary sources include the following kinds of materials:

- Books written based on primary materials about the period
- Books written based on primary materials about persons who played a major role in the events under consideration
- Books and articles written based on primary materials about the culture, the social norms, the language, and the values of the period
- Quotations from primary sources
- Statistical data on the period
- The conclusions and inferences of other historians
- Multiple interpretations of the ethos of the time

Guidelines for the use of secondary sources:

1. Do not rely upon only a single secondary source.
2. Check facts and interpretations against primary sources whenever possible.
3. Accept the conclusions of other historians critically.
4. Place greatest reliance on secondary sources created by the best and most respected scholars.
5. Do not use the inferences of other scholars as if they were facts.
6. Ensure that you recognize any bias the writer brings to his/her interpretation of history.
7. Understand the primary point of the book as a basis for evaluating the value of the material presented in it to your questions.

COMPETENCY 5.0   USE READING STRATEGIES TO COMPREHEND WRITTEN MATERIAL

Skill 5.1   Organize and summarizing information

Sample Passage

Chili peppers may turn out to be the wonder drug of the decade. The fiery fruit comes in many sizes, shapes, and colors, all of which grow on plants that are genetic descendants of the tepin plant, originally native to the Americas. Connoisseurs of the regional cuisines of the Southwest and Louisiana are already well aware that food flavored with chilies can cause a good sweat, but medical researchers are learning more every day about the medical power of capsaicin, the ingredient in the peppers that produces the heat.

Capsaicin as a pain medication has been a part of folk medicine for centuries. It is, in fact, the active ingredient in several currently available over-the-counter liniments for sore muscles. Recent research has been examining the value of the compound for the treatment of other painful conditions. Capsaicin shows some promise in the treatment of phantom limb syndrome, as well as shingles and some types of headaches. Additional research focuses upon the use of capsaicin to relieve pain in post-surgical patients. Scientists speculate that application of the compound to the skin causes the body to release endorphins—natural pain relievers manufactured by the body itself. An alternative theory holds that capsaicin somehow interferes with the transmission of signals along the nerve fibers, thus reducing the sensation of pain.

In addition to its well-documented history as a painkiller, capsaicin has recently received attention as a phytochemical, one of the naturally occurring compounds from foods that show cancer-fighting qualities. Like the phytochemical sulfoaphane found in broccoli, capsaicin might turn out to be an agent capable of short-circuiting the actions of carcinogens at the cell level before they can cause cancer.

Summary: Chili peppers contain a chemical called capsaicin that has proved useful in treating a variety of ailments. Recent research reveals that capsaicin is a phytochemical, a natural compound that may help fight cancer.

Outline: -Chili peppers could be the wonder drug of the decade.
-Chili peppers contain capsaicin.
-Capsaicin can be used as a pain medication.
-Capsaicin is a phytochemical.
-Phytochemicals show cancer-fighting qualities.
-Capsaicin might be able to short-circuit the effects of carcinogens.

Skill 5.2   Follow written instructions or directions

Step by Step

How does one get from here to there, from kindergarten to graduate school or to a trade school? The answer of course is by one step at a time, by carefully organizing one's courses of action, each phase building on the previous step and leading to the next.

Similarly, when taking a test and you are asked to follow written instructions or directions, the examiner wants to see how you manage your answer to the exam question. How do you organize your answer logically? How do you support your conclusions? How well connected are your ideas and the support you bring to your argument?

Look at how the writer does these tasks in the following essay:

Parenting Classes

Someone once said that the two most difficult jobs in the world—voting and being a parent—are given to rank amateurs. The consequences of this inequity are voter apathy and inept parenting, leading to, on the one hand, an apparent failure of the democratic process and, on the other hand, misbehaving and misguided children.

The antidote for the first problem is in place in most school systems. Classes in history, civics, history, government, and student government provide a kind of "hands on" training in becoming an active member of society so that the step from studenthood to citizenship is clear and expected.

On the other hand, most school systems in the past have avoided or given only lip service to the issue of parenting and parenting skills. The moral issue of illegitimate births aside, the reality of the world is that each year there are large numbers of children born to unwed parents who have had little, or no, training in child rearing.

What was done on the farm in the past is irrelevant here—the farm is gone and/or has been replaced by the inner city, and the pressing issue is how to train uneducated new parents in the child rearing tasks before them. Other issues are secondary to the immediate needs of newborns and their futures. And it is in their futures that the quality of life for all of us is found.

Thus, while we can debate this issue all we wish, we cannot responsibly ignore that uneducated parents need to be educated in the tasks before them, and it is clear that the best way to do this is in the school system, where these new parents are already learning how to be responsible citizens in the civics and other classes currently in place.

Notice how the writer moves sequentially from one idea to the next, maintaining throughout the parallel of citizenship and parenthood, from the opening quotation, paragraph by paragraph to the concluding sentence. Each idea is developed from the preceding idea, and each new idea refers to the preceding ideas. At no point do related, but irrelevant, issues sidetrack the writer.

Skill 5.3   Interpret information presented in charts, graphs, or tables

See Skill 9.2.

COMPETENCY 6.0   DETERMINE THE MEANING OF WORDS AND PHRASES

Skill 6.1   Determine the meaning of words and phrases in context

Context clues help readers determine the meaning of words with which they are not familiar. The context of a word is the sentence or sentences that surround the word.

Read the following sentences and attempt to determine the meanings of the words in bold print.

> The **luminosity** of the room was so incredible that there was no need for lights.

> > If there was no need for lights then one must assume that the word *luminosity* has something to do with giving off light. The definition of *luminosity* is "the emission of light."

> Jamie could not understand Joe's feelings. His mood swings made understanding him somewhat of an **enigma.**

> > The fact that he could not be understood made him somewhat of a puzzle. The definition of *enigma* is "a mystery or puzzle."

Familiarity with word roots (the basic elements of words) and with prefixes can help one determine the meanings of unknown words.

Following is a partial list of roots and prefixes. It might be useful to review these.

Root	Meaning	Example
aqua	water	aqualung
astro	stars	astrology
bio	life	biology
carn	meat	carnivorous
circum	around	circumnavigate
geo	earth	geology
herb	plant	herbivorous
mal	bad	malicious
neo	new	neonatal
tele	distant	telescope

Prefix	Meaning	Example
un-	not	unnamed
re-	again	reenter
il-	not	illegible
pre-	before	preset
mis-	incorrectly	misstate
in-	not	informal
anti-	against	antiwar
de-	opposite	derail
post-	after	postwar
ir-	not	irresponsible

Word forms

Sometimes a very familiar word can appear as a different part of speech.

You may have heard that *fraud* involves a criminal misrepresentation, so when it appears as the adjective form *fraudulent* ("He was suspected of fraudulent activities"), you can make an educated guess. You probably know that something out-of-date is *obsolete;* therefore, when you read about "built-in *obsolescence,*" you can detect the meaning of the unfamiliar word.

Practice questions: Read the following sentences and attempt to determine the meanings of the underlined words.

1. Farmer John got a two-horse plow and went to work. Straight <u>furrows</u> stretched out behind him.

   The word <u>furrows</u> means

   (A) long cuts made by a plow
   (B) vast, open fields
   (C) rows of corn
   (D) pairs of hitched horses

2. The survivors struggled ahead, <u>shambling</u> through the terrible cold, doing their best not to fall.

   The word <u>shambling</u> means

   (A) frozen in place
   (B) running
   (C) shivering uncontrollably
   (D) walking awkwardly

Answers:

1. (A) is the correct answer. The words *straight* and the expression *stretched out behind him* are your clues.

2. (D) is the correct answer. The words *ahead* and *through* are your clues.

The context for a word is the written passage that surrounds it. Sometimes the writer offers synonyms—words that have nearly the same meaning. Context clues can appear within the sentence itself, within the preceding and/or following sentence(s), or in the passage as a whole.

Sentence clues

Often, a writer will actually **define** a difficult or particularly important word for you the first time it appears in a passage. Phrases such as *that is, such as, which is,* or *is called* might announce the writer's intention to give just the definition you need. Occasionally, a writer will simply use a synonym (a word that means the same thing) or near-synonym joined by the word *or.* Look at the following examples:

> The <u>credibility</u>, that is to say the believability, of the witness was called into question by evidence of previous perjury.
> Nothing would <u>assuage</u>, or lessen, the child's grief.

Punctuation at the sentence level is often a clue to the meaning of a word. Commas, parentheses, quotation marks, and dashes tell the reader that the writer is offering a definition.

> A tendency toward <u>hyperbole</u>, extravagant exaggeration, is a common flaw among persuasive writers.

> Political <u>apathy</u>— lack of interest—can lead to the death of the state.

A writer might simply give an **explanation** in other words that you can understand in the same sentence:

> The <u>xenophobic</u> townspeople were suspicious of every foreigner.

Writers also explain a word in terms of its opposite at the sentence level:

> His <u>incarceration</u> was ended, and he was elated to be out of jail.

Adjacent sentence clues

The context for a word goes beyond the sentence in which it appears. At times, the writer uses adjacent (adjoining) sentences to present an explanation or definition:

The 200 dollars for the car repair would have to come out of the <u>contingency</u> fund. Fortunately, Angela's father had taught her to keep some money set aside for just such emergencies.

Analysis: The second sentence offers a clue to the definition of *contingency* as used in this sentence—"emergencies." Therefore, a fund for contingencies would be money tucked away for unforeseen and/or urgent events.

Entire passage clues

On occasion, you must look at an entire paragraph or passage to figure out the definition of a word or term. In the following paragraph, notice how the word *nostalgia* undergoes a form of extended definition throughout the selection rather than in just one sentence.

The word <u>nostalgia</u> links Greek words for "away from home" and "pain." If you are feeling <u>nostalgic,</u> then, you are probably in some physical distress or discomfort, suffering from a feeling of alienation and separation from loved ones or loved places. <u>Nostalgia</u> is that awful feeling you remember the first time you went away to camp or spent the weekend with a friend's family—homesickness, or some condition even more painful than that. But in common use, <u>nostalgia</u> has come to have associations that are more sentimental. A few years back, for example, a <u>nostalgia</u> craze had to do with the 1950s. We resurrected poodle skirts and saddle shoes, built new restaurants to look like old ones, and tried to make chicken à la king just as Mother probably never made it. In TV situation comedies, we recreated a pleasant world that probably never existed and relished our <u>nostalgia,</u> longing for a homey, comfortable lost time.

Skill 6.2   Determine the meaning of figurative expressions in context

1. Simile: direct comparison between two things. "My love is like a red-red rose."

2. Metaphor: indirect comparison between two things; the use of a word or phrase denoting one kind of object or action in place of another to suggest a comparison between them. While poets use them extensively, they are also integral to everyday speech. For example, chairs are said to have "legs" and "arms" although we know that it is humans and other animals that have these appendages.

3. Parallelism: the arrangement of ideas in phrases, sentences, and paragraphs that balance one element with another of equal importance and similar wording. An example from Francis Bacon's *Of Studies:* "Reading maketh a full man, conference a ready man, and writing an exact man."

4. Personification: human characteristics are attributed to an inanimate object, an abstract quality, or animal. Examples: John Bunyan wrote characters named Death, Knowledge, Giant Despair, Sloth, and Piety in his *Pilgrim's Progress.* The metaphor of "an arm of a chair" is a form of personification.

5. Euphemism: the substitution of an agreeable or inoffensive term for one that might offend or suggest something unpleasant. Many euphemisms, such as "passed away"; "crossed over"; or nowadays, "passed"; are used to refer to death to avoid using the real word.

6. Hyperbole: deliberate exaggeration for effect or comic effect. An example from Shakespeare's *The Merchant of Venice*:

    > Why, if two gods should play some heavenly match
    >
    > And on the wager lay two earthly women,
    >
    > And Portia one, there must be something else
    >
    > Pawned with the other, for the poor rude world
    >
    > Hath not her fellow.

7. Climax: a number of phrases or sentences are arranged in ascending order of rhetorical forcefulness. Example from Melville's *Moby Dick*:

    > All that most maddens and torments; all that
    > stirs up the lees of things; all truth with malice in it; all
    > that cracks the sinews and cakes the brain; all the
    > subtle demonisms of life and thought; all evil, to crazy

Ahab, were visibly personified and made practically assailable in Moby Dick.

8. Bathos: a ludicrous attempt to portray pathos—that is, to evoke pity, sympathy, or sorrow. It may result from inappropriately dignifying the commonplace, elevated language to describe something trivial, or greatly exaggerated pathos.

9. Oxymoron: a contradiction in terms deliberately employed for effect. It is usually seen in a qualifying adjective whose meaning is contrary to that of the noun it modifies, such as "wise folly."

10. Irony: expressing something other than and particularly opposite the literal meaning, such as words of praise when blame is intended. In poetry, it is often used as a sophisticated or resigned awareness of contrast between what is and what ought to be and expresses a controlled pathos without sentimentality. It is a form of indirection that avoids overt praise or censure—an early example: the Greek comic character Eiron, a clever underdog who by his wit repeatedly triumphs over the boastful character Alazon.

10. Alliteration: the repetition of consonant sounds in two or more neighboring words or syllables. In its simplest form, it reinforces one or two consonant sounds; example, Shakespeare's Sonnet #12: "When I do count the clock that tells the time."

Some poets have used more complex patterns of alliteration by creating consonants both at the beginning of words and at the beginning of stressed syllables within words; example, Shelley's "Stanzas Written in Dejection Near Naples": " The City's voice itself is soft like Solitude's."

11. Onomatopoeia: the naming of a thing or action by a vocal imitation of the sound associated with it, such as *buzz* or *hiss* or the use of words whose sound suggests the sense; a good example from "The Brook" by Tennyson:

> I chatter over stony ways,
>
> In little sharps and trebles,
>
> I bubble into eddying bays,
>
> I babble on the pebbles.

Sample Test: Reading

Read the passages and answer the questions that follow.

This writer has often been asked to tutor hospitalized children with cystic fibrosis. While undergoing all the precautionary measures to see these children (i.e. scrubbing thoroughly and donning sterilized protective gear for the child's protection), she has often wondered why their parents subject these children to the pressures of schooling and trying to catch up on what they have missed because of hospitalization, which is a normal part of cystic fibrosis patients' lives. These children undergo so many tortuous treatments a day that it seems cruel to expect them to learn as normal children do, especially with their life expectancies being as short as they are.

1. **What is the main idea of this passage?**
   (Average Rigor) (Skill 1.1)

   A. There is a lot of preparation involved in visiting a patient with cystic fibrosis.
   B. Children with cystic fibrosis are incapable of living normal lives.
   C. Certain concessions should be made for children with cystic fibrosis.
   D. Children with cystic fibrosis die young.

2. **How is the author so familiar with the procedures used when visiting a child with cystic fibrosis?**
   (Easy) (Skill 1.3)

   A. She has read about it.
   B. She works in a hospital.
   C. She is the parent of one.
   D. She often tutors them.

3. **What is the author's purpose?**
   (Rigorous) (Skill 2.1)

   A. To inform
   B. To entertain
   C. To describe
   D. To narrate

4. **What is the author's tone?**
   (Average Rigor) (Skill 2.4)

   A. Sympathetic
   B. Cruel
   C. Disbelieving
   D. Cheerful

5. **What type of organizational pattern is the author using?**
   (Rigorous) (Skill 3.2)

   A. Classification
   B. Explanation
   C. Comparison and contrast
   D. Cause and effect

6. What kind of relationship is found within the last sentence that starts with "These children undergo..." and ends with "...as short as they are"?
(Rigorous) (Skill 3.2)

   A. Addition
   B. Explanation
   C. Generalization
   D. Classification

7. Does the author present an argument that is valid or invalid concerning the schooling of children with cystic fibrosis?
(Rigorous) (Skill 4.1)

   A. Valid
   B. Invalid

8. The author states that it is "cruel" to expect children with cystic fibrosis to learn as "normal" children do. Is this a fact or an opinion?
(Average Rigor) (Skill 4.4)

   A. Fact
   B. Opinion

9. Is there evidence of bias in this paragraph?
(Rigorous) (Skill 4.5)

   A. Yes
   B. No

10. What is meant by the word *precautionary* in the second sentence?
(Average Rigor) (Skill 6.1)

    A. Careful
    B. Protective
    C. Medical
    D. Sterilizing

Disciplinary practices have been found to affect diverse areas of child development such as the acquisition of moral values, obedience to authority, and performance at school. Even though the dictionary has a specific definition of the word *discipline*, it is still open to interpretation by people of different cultures.

There are four types of disciplinary styles: assertion of power, withdrawal of love, reasoning, and permissiveness. Assertion of power involves the use of force to discourage unwanted behavior. Withdrawal of love involves making the love of a parent conditional on a child's good behavior. Reasoning involves persuading the child to behave one way rather than another. Permissiveness involves allowing the child to do as he or she pleases and face the consequences of his/her actions.

11. **What is the main idea of this passage? (Average Rigor) (Skill 1.2)**

    A. Different people have different ideas of what discipline is.
    B. Permissiveness is the most widely used disciplinary style.
    C. Most people agree on their definition of discipline.
    D. There are four disciplinary styles.

12. **Name the four types of disciplinary styles. (Easy) (Skill 1.3)**

    A. Reasoning, power assertion, morality, and permissiveness.
    B. Morality, reasoning, permissiveness, and withdrawal of love.
    C. Withdrawal of love, permissiveness, assertion of power, and reasoning.
    D. Permissiveness, morality, reasoning, and power assertion.

13. **What does the technique of reasoning involve? (Easy) (Skill 1.3)**

    A. Persuading the child to behave in a certain way.
    B. Allowing the child to do as he/she pleases.
    C. Using force to discourage unwanted behavior.
    D. Making love conditional on good behavior.

14. **What is the author's purpose in writing this? (Easy) (Skill 2.1)**

    A. To describe
    B. To narrate
    C. To entertain
    D. To inform

15. **What is the author's tone? (Average Rigor) (Skill 2.4)**

   A.   Disbelieving
   B.   Angry
   C.   Informative
   D.   Optimistic

16. **What organizational structure is used in the first sentence of the second paragraph? (Rigorous) (Skill 3.2)**

   A.   Addition
   B.   Explanation
   C.   Definition
   D.   Simple listing

17. **What is the overall organizational pattern of this passage? (Rigorous) (Skill 3.2)**

   A.   Generalization
   B.   Cause and effect
   C.   Addition
   D.   Summary

18. **From reading this passage, we can conclude that (Rigorous) (Skill 3.5)**

   A.   The author is a teacher.
   B.   The author has many children.
   C.   The author has written a book about discipline.
   D.   The author has done a lot of research on discipline.

19. **The author states that "assertion of power involves the use of force to discourage unwanted behavior." Is this a fact or an opinion? (Average Rigor) (Skill 4.4)**

   A.   Fact
   B.   Opinion

20. **Is this passage biased? (Rigorous) (Skill 4.5)**

   A.   Yes
   B.   No

21. **What is the meaning of the word *diverse* in the first sentence? (Easy) (Skill 6.1)**

   A.   Many
   B.   Related to children
   C.   Disciplinary
   D.   Moral

One of the most difficult problems plaguing American education is the assessment of teachers. No one denies that teachers ought to be answerable for what they do, but what exactly does that mean? The Oxford American Dictionary defines accountability as "the obligation to give a reckoning or explanation for one's actions."

Does a student have to learn for teaching to have taken place? Historically, teaching has not been defined in this restrictive manner; the teacher was thought to be responsible for the quantity and quality of material covered and the way in which it was presented. However, some definitions of teaching now imply that students must learn in order for teaching to have taken place.

As a teacher who tries my best to keep current on all the latest teaching strategies, I believe that those teachers who do not bother even to pick up an educational journal every once in a while should be kept under close watch. Many teachers out there have been teaching for decades and refuse to change their ways even if research has proven that their methods are outdated and ineffective. There is no place in the profession of teaching for these types of individuals. It is time that the American educational system clean house, for the sake of our children.

22. **What is the main idea of the passage? (Average Rigor) (Skill 1.1)**

   A. Teachers should not be answerable for what they do.
   B. Teachers who do not do their job should be fired.
   C. The author is a good teacher.
   D. Assessment of teachers is a serious problem in society today.

23. **The author states that teacher assessment is a problem for (Easy) (Skill 1.3)**

   A. Elementary schools
   B. Secondary schools
   C. American education
   D. Families

24. **Where does the author get her definition of *accountability*? (Easy) (Skill 1.3)**

   A. Webster's Dictionary
   B. Encyclopedia Britannica
   C. Oxford Dictionary
   D. World Book Encyclopedia

25. **What is the author's purpose in writing this? (Average Rigor) (Skill 2.1)**

    A.   To entertain
    B.   To narrate
    C.   To describe
    D.   To persuade

26. **The author's tone is one of (Average Rigor) (Skill 2.3)**

    A.   Disbelief
    B.   Excitement
    C.   Support
    D.   Concern

27. **What is the organizational pattern of the second paragraph? (Rigorous) (Skill 3.2)**

    A.   Cause and effect
    B.   Classification
    C.   Addition
    D.   Explanation

28. **What is the author's overall organizational pattern? (Rigorous) (Skill 3.2)**

    A.   Classification
    B.   Cause and effect
    C.   Definition
    D.   Comparison and Contrast

29. **From the passage, one can infer that (Rigorous) (Skill 3.5)**

    A.   The author considers herself a good teacher.
    B.   Poor teachers will be fired.
    C.   Students have to learn for teaching to take place.
    D.   The author will be fired.

30. **Is this a valid argument? (Rigorous) (Skill 4.1)**

    A.   Yes
    B.   No

31. **Teachers who do not keep current on educational trends should be fired. Is this a fact or an opinion? (Average Rigor) (Skill 4.4)**

    A.   Fact
    B.   Opinion

32. **Is there evidence of bias in this passage? (Rigorous) (Skill 4.5)**

    A.   Yes
    B.   No

33. **What is the meaning of the word *reckoning* in the third sentence? (Average Rigor) (Skill 6.1)**

    A.   Thought
    B.   Answer
    C.   Obligation
    D.   Explanation

34. **What is meant by the word *plaguing* in the first sentence? (Easy) (Skill 6.1)**

   A. Causing problems
   B. Causing illness
   C. Causing anger
   D. Causing failure

Mr. Smith gave instructions for the painting to be hung on the wall. And then it leaped forth before his eyes—the little cottages on the river, the white clouds floating over the valley, and the green of the towering mountain ranges, which were seen in the distance. The painting was so vivid that it seemed almost real. Mr. Smith was now certain that the painting had been the worth money.

35. **What is the main idea of this passage? (Average Rigor) (Skill 1.1)**

   A. The painting that Mr. Smith purchased is expensive.
   B. Mr. Smith purchased a painting.
   C. Mr. Smith was pleased with the quality of the painting he had purchased.
   D. The painting depicted cottages and valleys.

36. **The author's purpose is to (Rigorous) (Skill 2.1)**

   A. Inform
   B. Entertain
   C. Persuade
   D. Narrate

37. **From the last sentence, one can infer that (Rigorous) (Skill 3.5)**

   A. The painting was expensive.
   B. The painting was inexpensive.
   C. Mr. Smith was considering purchasing the painting.
   D. Mr. Smith thought the painting was too expensive and decided not to purchase it.

38. **Is this passage biased? (Rigorous) (Skill 4.5)**

   A. Yes
   B. No

39. **What is the meaning of the word *vivid* in the third sentence? (Average Rigor) (Skill 6.1)**

   A. Lifelike
   B. Dark
   C. Expensive
   D. Big

40. **What does the author mean by the expression "it leaped forth before his eyes?" (Average Rigor) (Skill 6.2)**

   A. The painting fell off the wall.
   B. The painting appeared so real, it was almost three-dimensional.
   C. The painting struck Mr. Smith in the face.
   D. Mr. Smith was hallucinating.

Chili peppers may turn out to be the wonder drug of the decade. The fiery fruit comes in many sizes, shapes, and colors, all of which grow on plants that are genetic descendants of the tepin plant, originally native to the Americas. Connoisseurs of the regional cuisines of the Southwest and Louisiana are already well aware that food flavored with chilies can cause a good sweat, but medical researchers are learning more every day about the medical power of capsaicin, the ingredient in the peppers that produces the heat.

Capsaicin as a pain medication has been a part of folk medicine for centuries. It is, in fact, the active ingredient in several currently available over-the-counter liniments for sore muscles. Recent research has been examining the value of the compound for the treatment of other painful conditions. Capsaicin shows some promise in the treatment of phantom limb syndrome, as well as shingles, and some types of headaches. Additional research focuses upon the use of capsaicin to relieve pain in post-surgical patients. Scientists speculate that application of the compound to the skin causes the body to release endorphins—natural pain relievers manufactured by the body itself. An alternative theory holds that capsaicin somehow interferes with the transmission of signals along the nerve fibers, thus reducing the sensation of pain.

In addition to its well-documented history as a painkiller, capsaicin has recently received attention as a phytochemical, one of the naturally occurring compounds from foods that show cancer-fighting qualities. Like the phytochemical sulfoaphane found in broccoli, capsaicin might turn out to be an agent capable of short-circuiting the actions of carcinogens at the cell level before they can cause cancer.

41. **All of the following medical problems have been treated using capsaicin EXCEPT:**

    (Average Rigor) (Skill 1.3)

    A.   cancer
    B.   shingles
    C.   sore muscles
    D.   headache

42. **The author's primary purpose is to:**

    (Average Rigor) (Skill 2.1)

    A.   entertain the reader with unusual stories about chilies
    B.   narrate the story of the discovery of capsaicin
    C.   describe the medicinal properties of the tepin plant
    D.   inform the reader of the medical research about capsaicin

Answer Key: Reading

1. C.
2. D.
3. C.
4. A.
5. B.
6. B.
7. B.
8. B.
9. A.
10. B.
11. A.
12. C.
13. A.
14. D.
15. C.
16. D.
17. C.
18. D.
19. A.
20. B.
21. A.
22. D.
23. C.
24. C.
25. D.
26. D.
27. D.
28. C.
29. A.
30. B.
31. B.
32. A.
33. D.
34. A.
35. C.
36. D.
37. A.
38. B.
39. A.
40. B.
41. A.
42. D.

Rigor Table: Reading

	Easy 20%	Average 40%	Rigorous 40%
Questions (42)	2, 12, 13, 14, 21, 23, 24, 34	1, 4, 8, 10, 11, 15, 19, 22, 25, 26, 31, 33, 35, 39, 40, 41, 42	3, 5, 6, 7, 9, 16, 17, 18, 20, 27, 28, 29, 30, 32, 36, 37, 38
TOTALS	8 (19%)	17 (40.5%)	17 (40.5%)

Rationales with Sample Questions: Reading

Read the passages and answer the questions that follow.

This writer has often been asked to tutor hospitalized children with cystic fibrosis. While undergoing all the precautionary measures to see these children (i.e. scrubbing thoroughly and donning sterilized protective gear for the child's protection), she has often wondered why their parents subject these children to the pressures of schooling and trying to catch up on what they have missed because of hospitalization, which is a normal part of cystic fibrosis patients' lives. These children undergo so many tortuous treatments a day that it seems cruel to expect them to learn as normal children do, especially with their life expectancies being as short as they are.

1.   **What is the main idea of this passage?**
        (Average Rigor) (Skill 1.1)

        A.   There is a lot of preparation involved in visiting a patient with cystic fibrosis.
        B.   Children with cystic fibrosis are incapable of living normal lives.
        C.   Certain concessions should be made for children with cystic fibrosis.
        D.   Children with cystic fibrosis die young.

Answer: C. Certain concessions should be made for children with cystic fibrosis.

The author states that she wonders, "why parents subject these children to the pressures of schooling" and that "it seems cruel to expect them to learn as normal children do." In making these statements she appears to be expressing the belief that these children should not have to do what "normal" children do. They have enough to deal with—the illness itself.

2.   **How is the author so familiar with the procedures used when visiting a child with cystic fibrosis?**
        (Easy) (Skill 1.3)

        A.   She has read about it.
        B.   She works in a hospital.
        C.   She is the parent of one.
        D.   She often tutors them.

Answer: D. She often tutors them.

The writer states this fact in the opening sentence.

3. **What is the author's purpose?**
   (Rigorous) (Skill 2.1)

    A.   To inform
    B.   To entertain
    C.   To describe
    D.   To narrate

Answer: C. To describe

The author is simply describing her experience in working with children with cystic fibrosis.

4. **What is the author's tone?**
   (Average Rigor) (Skill 2.4)

    A.   Sympathetic
    B.   Cruel
    C.   Disbelieving
    D.   Cheerful

Answer: A. Sympathetic

The author states, "It seems cruel to expect them to learn as normal children do," thereby indicating that she feels sorry for them.

5. **What type of organizational pattern is the author using?**
   (Rigorous) (Skill 3.2)

    A.   Classification
    B.   Explanation
    C.   Comparison and
          contrast
    D.   Cause and effect

Answer: B. Explanation

The author mentions tutoring children with cystic fibrosis in her opening sentence and goes on to "explain" some of the issues that are involved with her job.

6. **What kind of relationship is found within the last sentence which starts with "These children undergo..." and ends with "...as short as they are"?**
    (Rigorous) (Skill 3.2)

    A. Addition
    B. Explanation
    C. Generalization
    D. Classification

Answer: B. Explanation

In mentioning that their life expectancies are short, she is explaining by giving one reason why it is cruel to expect them to learn as normal children do.

7. **Does the author present an argument that is valid or invalid concerning the schooling of children with cystic fibrosis?**
    (Rigorous) (Skill 4.1)

    A. Valid
    B. Invalid

Answer: B. Invalid

Even though the writer's argument makes good sense to most readers, it shows bias and lacks real evidence.

8. **The author states that it is *cruel* to expect children with cystic fibrosis to learn as *normal* children do. Is this a fact or an opinion?**
    (Average Rigor) (Skill 4.4)

    A. Fact
    B. Opinion

Answer: B. Opinion

The fact that she states that it *seems* cruel indicates there is no evidence to support this belief.

9.   **Is there evidence of bias in this paragraph?**
        (Rigorous) (Skill 4.5)

        A.   Yes
        B.   No

Answer: A. Yes

The writer clearly feels sorry for these children and gears her writing in that direction.

10.   **What is meant by the word *precautionary* in the second sentence?**
        (Average Rigor) (Skill 6.1)

        A.   Careful
        B.   Protective
        C.   Medical
        D.   Sterilizing

Answer: B. Protective

The writer uses expressions such as *protective gear* and *child's protection* to emphasize this.

Disciplinary practices have been found to affect diverse areas of child development such as the acquisition of moral values, obedience to authority, and performance at school. Even though the dictionary has a specific definition of the word *discipline*, it is still open to interpretation by people of different cultures.

There are four types of disciplinary styles: assertion of power, withdrawal of love, reasoning, and permissiveness. Assertion of power involves the use of force to discourage unwanted behavior. Withdrawal of love involves making the love of a parent conditional on a child's good behavior. Reasoning involves persuading the child to behave one way rather than another. Permissiveness involves allowing the child to do as he or she pleases and face the consequences of his/her actions.

11.   What is the main idea of this passage?
(Average Rigor) (Skill 1.2)

    A.   Different people have different ideas of what discipline is.
    B.   Permissiveness is the most widely used disciplinary style.
    C.   Most people agree on their definition of discipline.
    D.   There are four disciplinary styles.

Answer: A. Different people have different ideas of what discipline is.

Choice C is not true; the opposite is stated in the passage. Choice B could be true, but we have no evidence of this. Choice D is just one of the many facts listed in the passage.

12.   Name the four types of disciplinary styles.
(Easy) (Skill 1.3)

    A.   Reasoning, power assertion, morality, and permissiveness
    B.   Morality, reasoning, permissiveness, and withdrawal of love
    C.   Withdrawal of love, permissiveness, assertion of power, and reasoning
    D.   Permissiveness, morality, reasoning, and power assertion

Answer: C. Withdrawal of love, permissiveness, assertion of power, and reasoning.

This is directly stated in the second paragraph.

13.   What does the technique of reasoning involve?
(Easy) (Skill 1.3)

    A.   Persuading the child to behave in a certain way
    B.   Allowing the child to do as he/she pleases
    C.   Using force to discourage unwanted behavior
    D.   Making love conditional on good behavior

Answer: A. Persuading the child to behave in a certain way.

This fact is directly stated in the second paragraph.

14. **What is the author's purpose in writing this?**
(Easy) (Skill 2.1)

   A.   To describe
   B.   To narrate
   C.   To entertain
   D.   To inform

Answer: D. To inform

The author is providing the reader with information about disciplinary practices.

15. **What is the author's tone?**
(Average Rigor) (Skill 2.4)

   A.   Disbelieving
   B.   Angry
   C.   Informative
   D.   Optimistic

Answer: C. Informative

The author appears simply to be stating the facts.

16. **What organizational structure is used in the first sentence of the second paragraph?**
(Rigorous) (Skill 3.2)

   A.   Addition
   B.   Explanation
   C.   Definition
   D.   Simple listing

Answer: D. Simple Listing

The author simply states the types of disciplinary styles.

17.   **What is the overall organizational pattern of this passage? (Rigorous) (Skill 3.2)**

   A.   Generalization
   B.   Cause and effect
   C.   Addition
   D.   Summary

Answer: C. Addition

The author has taken a subject, in this case discipline, and developed it point by point.

18.   **From reading this passage, we can conclude that (Rigorous) (Skill 3.5)**

   A.   The author is a teacher.
   B.   The author has many children.
   C.   The author has written a book about discipline.
   D.   The author has done a lot of research on discipline.

Answer: D. The author has done a lot of research on discipline.

Given all the facts mentioned in the passage, this is the only inference one can make.

19.   **The author states "assertion of power involves the use of force to discourage unwanted behavior." Is this a fact or an opinion? (Average Rigor) (Skill 4.4)**

   A.   Fact
   B.   Opinion

Answer: A. Fact

The author appears to have done extensive research on this subject.

20.   **Is this passage biased? (Rigorous) (Skill 4.5)**

   A.   Yes
   B.   No

Answer: B. No

If the reader were so inclined, he could research discipline and find this information.

21. **What is the meaning of the word *diverse* in the first sentence? (Easy) (Skill 6.1)**

    A.   Many
    B.   Related to children
    C.   Disciplinary
    D.   Moral

Answer: A. Many

Any of the other choices would be redundant in this sentence.

One of the most difficult problems plaguing American education is the assessment of teachers. No one denies that teachers ought to be answerable for what they do, but what exactly does that mean? The Oxford American Dictionary defines accountability as "the obligation to give a reckoning or explanation for one's actions."

Does a student have to learn for teaching to have taken place? Historically, teaching has not been defined in this restrictive manner; the teacher was thought to be responsible for the quantity and quality of material covered and the way in which it was presented. However, some definitions of teaching now imply that students must learn in order for teaching to have taken place.

As a teacher who tries my best to keep current on all the latest teaching strategies, I believe that those teachers who do not bother even to pick up an educational journal every once in a while should be kept under close watch. Many teachers out there have been teaching for decades and refuse to change their ways even if research has proven that their methods are outdated and ineffective. There is no place in the profession of teaching for these types of individuals. It is time that the American educational system clean house, for the sake of our children.

22.   **What is the main idea of the passage?**
       (Average Rigor) (Skill 1.1)

       A.   Teachers should not be answerable for what they do.
       B.   Teachers who do not do their job should be fired.
       C.   The author is a good teacher.
       D.   Assessment of teachers is a serious problem in society today.

Answer: D. Assessment of teachers is a serious problem in society today.

Most of the passage is dedicated to elaborating on why teacher assessment is such a problem.

23.   **The author states that teacher assessment is a problem for**
       (Easy) (Skill 1.3)

       A.   Elementary schools
       B.   Secondary schools
       C.   American education
       D.   Families

Answer: C. American education

This fact is directly stated in the first paragraph.

24.   **Where does the author get her definition of *accountability*?**
       (Easy) (Skill 1.3)

       A.   Webster's Dictionary
       B.   Encyclopedia Britannica
       C.   Oxford Dictionary
       D.   World Book Encyclopedia

Answer: C. Oxford Dictionary

This is directly stated in the third sentence of the first paragraph.

25. **What is the author's purpose in writing this?**
(Average Rigor) (Skill 2.1)

   A.   To entertain
   B.   To narrate
   C.   To describe
   D.   To persuade

Answer: D. To persuade

The author does some describing, but the majority of her statements seem geared towards convincing the reader that teachers who are lazy or who do not keep current should be fired.

26. **The author's tone is one of**
(Average Rigor) (Skill 2.3)

   A.   Disbelief
   B.   Excitement
   C.   Support
   D.   Concern

Answer: D. Concern

The author appears concerned with the future of education.

27. **What is the organizational pattern of the second paragraph?**
(Rigorous) (Skill 3.2)

   A.   Cause and effect
   B.   Classification
   C.   Addition
   D.   Explanation

Answer: D. Explanation

The author goes on to explain further what she meant by "...what exactly does that mean?" in the first paragraph.

28.   **What is the author's overall organizational pattern?**
        (Rigorous) (Skill 3.2)

        A.   Classification
        B.   Cause and effect
        C.   Definition
        D.   Comparison and Contrast

Answer: C. Definition

The author identifies teacher assessment as a problem and spends the rest of
the passage defining why it is considered a problem.

29.   **From the passage, one can infer that**
        (Rigorous) (Skill 3.5)

        A.   The author considers herself a good teacher.
        B.   Poor teachers will be fired.
        C.   Students have to learn for teaching to take place.
        D.   The author will be fired.

Answer: A. The author considers herself a good teacher.

The first sentence of the third paragraph alludes to this.

30.   **Is this a valid argument?**
        (Rigorous) (Skill 4.1)

        A.   Yes
        B.   No

Answer: B. No

In the third paragraph, the author appears to be resentful of lazy teachers.

31.   **Teachers who do not keep current on educational trends should be**
        fired. Is this a fact or an opinion?
        (Average Rigor) (Skill 4.4)

        A.   Fact
        B.   Opinion

Answer: B. Opinion

There may be those who feel they can be good teachers by using old methods.

32.   **Is there evidence of bias in this passage?**
       (Rigorous) (Skill 4.5)

       A.   Yes
       B.   No

Answer: A. Yes

The entire third paragraph is the author's opinion on the matter.

33.   **What is the meaning of the word *reckoning* in the third sentence?**
       (Average Rigor) (Skill 6.1)

       A.   Thought
       B.   Answer
       C.   Obligation
       D.   Explanation

Answer: D. Explanation

The meaning of this word is directly stated in the same sentence.

34.   **What is meant by the word *plaguing* in the first sentence?**
       (Easy) (Skill 6.1)

       A.   Causing problems
       B.   Causing illness
       C.   Causing anger
       D.   Causing failure

Answer: A. Causing problems

The first paragraph makes this definition clear.

       Mr. Smith gave instructions for the painting to be hung on the wall. Then it leaped forth before his eyes—the little cottages on the river, the white clouds floating over the valley, and the green of the towering mountain ranges, which were seen in the distance. The painting was so vivid that it seemed almost real. Mr. Smith was now certain that the painting had been worth the money.

35. **What is the main idea of this passage?**
(Average Rigor) (Skill 1.1)

A.   The painting that Mr. Smith purchased is expensive.
B.   Mr. Smith purchased a painting.
C.   Mr. Smith was pleased with the quality of the painting he had purchased.
D.   The painting depicted cottages and valleys.

Answer: C. Mr. Smith was pleased with the quality of the painting he had purchased.

Every sentence in the paragraph alludes to this fact.

36. **The author's purpose is to**
(Rigorous) (Skill 2.1)

A.   Inform
B.   Entertain
C.   Persuade
D.   Narrate

Answer: D. Narrate

The author is simply narrating or telling the story of Mr. Smith and his painting.

37. **From the last sentence, one can infer that**
(Rigorous) (Skill 3.5)

A.   The painting was expensive.
B.   The painting was inexpensive.
C.   Mr. Smith was considering purchasing the painting.
D.   Mr. Smith thought the painting was too expensive and decided not to purchase it.

Answer: A. The painting was expensive.

Choice B is incorrect because, had the painting been cheap, chances are that Mr. Smith would not have considered its purchase. Choices C and D are ruled out by the fact that the painting had already been purchased. The author makes this clear when she says, "...the painting had been worth the money."

38.   **Is this passage biased?**
       (Rigorous) (Skill 4.5)

       A.   Yes
       B.   No

Answer: B. No

The author appears just to be telling what happened when Mr. Smith had his new painting hung on the wall.

39.   **What is the meaning of the word *vivid* in the third sentence?**
       (Average Rigor) (Skill 6.1)

       A.   Lifelike
       B.   Dark
       C.   Expensive
       D.   Big

Answer: A. Lifelike

The second half of the same sentence reinforces this.

40.   **What does the author mean by the expression "it leaped forth before his eyes?"**
       (Average Rigor) (Skill 6.2)

       A.   The painting fell off the wall.
       B.   The painting appeared so real it was almost three-dimensional.
       C.   The painting struck Mr. Smith in the face.
       D.   Mr. Smith was hallucinating.

Answer: B. The painting appeared so real it was almost three-dimensional.

This is almost directly stated in the third sentence.

Chili peppers may turn out to be the wonder drug of the decade. The fiery fruit comes in many sizes, shapes, and colors, all of which grow on plants that are genetic descendants of the tepin plant, originally native to the Americas. Connoisseurs of the regional cuisines of the Southwest and Louisiana are already well aware that food flavored with chilies can cause a good sweat, but medical researchers are learning more every day about the medical power of capsaicin, the ingredient in the peppers that produces the heat.

Capsaicin as a pain medication has been a part of folk medicine for centuries. It is, in fact, the active ingredient in several currently available over-the-counter liniments for sore muscles. Recent research has been examining the value of the compound for the treatment of other painful conditions. Capsaicin shows some promise in the treatment of phantom limb syndrome, as well as shingles, and some types of headaches. Additional research focuses upon the use of capsaicin to relieve pain in post-surgical patients. Scientists speculate that application of the compound to the skin causes the body to release endorphins—natural pain relievers manufactured by the body itself. An alternative theory holds that capsaicin somehow interferes with the transmission of signals along the nerve fibers, thus reducing the sensation of pain.

In addition to its well-documented history as a painkiller, capsaicin has recently received attention as a phytochemical, one of the naturally occurring compounds from foods that show cancer-fighting qualities. Like the phytochemical sulfoaphane found in broccoli, capsaicin might turn out to be an agent capable of short-circuiting the actions of carcinogens at the cell level before they can cause cancer.

41.   **All of the following medical problems have been treated using capsaicin EXCEPT:**

   (Average Rigor) (Skill 1.3)

   A.   cancer
   B.   shingles
   C.   sore muscles
   D.   headache

Answer: A. cancer

Choice A is the exception. The passage states that capsaicin "might turn out to be" effective in fighting cancer, but actual cancer treatments with the drug are not mentioned.

42.   **The author's primary purpose is to:**

   (Average Rigor) (Skill 2.1)

   A.   entertain the reader with unusual stories about chilies
   B.   narrate the story of the discovery of capsaicin
   C.   describe the medicinal properties of the tepin plant
   D.   inform the reader of the medical research about capsaicin

Answer: D. inform the reader of the medical research about capsaicin.

This purpose is conveyed in the last sentence of paragraph one.

COMPETENCY 7.0   UNDERSTAND NUMBER PROPERTIES AND
                   NUMBER OPERATIONS

Skill 7.1   Identify mathematically equivalent ways of representing numbers

Rational numbers can be expressed as the ratio of two integers, where b ≠ 0, for example $\frac{2}{3}$, $-\frac{4}{5}$, $5 = \frac{5}{1}$.

The rational numbers include integers, fractions and mixed numbers, and terminating and repeating decimals. Every rational number can be expressed as a repeating or terminating decimal and can be shown on a number line.

Integers are positive and negative whole numbers and zero.
    ...-6, -5, -4, -3, -2, -1, 0, 1, 2, 3, 4, 5, 6,...

Whole numbers are natural numbers and zero.
    0, 1, 2, 3, 4, 5, 6...

Natural numbers are the counting numbers.
    1, 2, 3, 4, 5, 6...

Irrational numbers are real numbers that cannot be written as the ratio of two integers. These are infinite non-repeating decimals.
    <u>Examples</u>: $\sqrt{5}$ = 2.2360...   pi =∏ = 3.1415927...

A **fraction** is an expression of numbers in the form of x/y, where **x** is the numerator and **y** is the denominator, which cannot be zero.

Example: $\frac{3}{7}$ 3 is the numerator; 7 is the denominator

If the fraction has common factors for the numerator and denominator, divide both by the common factor to reduce the fraction to its lowest form.

Example:

$$\frac{13}{39} = \frac{1 \times 13}{3 \times 13} = \frac{1}{3}$$ Divide by the common factor 13

A **mixed** number has an integer part and a fractional part.

Example: $2\frac{1}{4}, \ ^-5\frac{1}{6}, \ 7\frac{1}{3}$

Percent = per 100 (written with the symbol %). Thus $10\% = \dfrac{10}{100} = \dfrac{1}{10}$.

Decimals = deci = part of ten. To find the decimal equivalent of a fraction, use the denominator to divide the numerator as shown in the following example.

Example: Find the decimal equivalent of $\dfrac{7}{10}$.

Since 10 cannot divide into 7 evenly

$$\frac{7}{10} = 0.7$$

The **exponent form** is a shortcut method to write repeated multiplication. Basic form: b^n, where b is called the base and n is the exponent. b and n are both real numbers. b^n implies that the base b is multiplied by itself n times.

Examples: $3^4 = 3 \times 3 \times 3 \times 3 = 81$

$2^3 = 2 \times 2 \times 2 = 8$

$(^-2)^4 = (^-2) \times (^-2) \times (^-2) \times (^-2) = 16$

$^-2^4 = ^- (2 \times 2 \times 2 \times 2) = ^- 16$

Key exponent rules:

For 'a' nonzero, and 'm' and 'n' real numbers:

1) $a^m \cdot a^n = a^{(m+n)}$ Product rule

2) $\dfrac{a^m}{a^n} = a^{(m-n)}$ Quotient rule

3) $\dfrac{a^{-m}}{a^{-n}} = \dfrac{a^n}{a^m}$

When 10 is raised to any power, the exponent tells the numbers of zeroes in the product.

Example: $10^7 = 10,000,000$

Caution: Unless the negative sign is inside the parentheses and the exponent is outside the parentheses, the sign is not affected by the exponent.

$(^-2)^4$ implies that -2 is multiplied by itself 4 times.

$^-2^4$ implies that 2 is multiplied by itself 4 times, then the answer is negated.

Scientific notation is a more convenient method for writing very large and very small numbers. It employs two factors. The first factor is a number between 1 and 10. The second factor is a power of 10. This notation is "shorthand" for expressing large numbers (such as the weight of 100 elephants) or small numbers (such as the weight of an atom in pounds).

Recall that:

$10^n = (10)^n$ Ten multiplied by itself n times.

$10^0 = 1$ Any nonzero number raised to power of zero is 1.

$10^1 = 10$

$10^2 = 10 \times 10 = 100$

$10^3 = 10 \times 10 \times 10 = 1000$ (kilo)

$10^{-1} = 1/10$ (deci)

$10^{-2} = 1/100$ (centi)

$10^{-3} = 1/1000$ (milli)

$10^{-6} = 1/1,000,000$ (micro)

Example: Write 46,368,000 in scientific notation.

1)   Introduce a decimal point and decimal places.
      46,368,000 = 46,368,000.0000

2)   Make a mark between the two digits that give a number between
      -9.9 and 9.9.
      4 ∧ 6,368,000 .0000

3)   Count the number of digit places between the decimal point and the
      ∧ mark. This number is the nth power of ten.

      So, $46,368,000 = 4.6368 \times 10^7$

Example: Write 0.00397 in scientific notation.

    1)   Decimal place is already in place.

    2)   Make a mark between 3 and 9 to get one number between -9.9 and 9.9.

    3)   Move decimal place to the mark (3 hops).

        $0.003 \wedge 97$

        Motion is to the right, so n of 10^n is negative.

        Therefore, $0.00397 = 3.97 \times 10^{-3}$

A **decimal** can be converted to a **percent** by multiplying by 100 or merely moving the decimal point two places to the right. A **percent** can be converted to a **decimal** by dividing by 100 or moving the decimal point two places to the left.

Examples: $0.375 = 37.5\%$
                 $0.7 = 70\%$
                 $0.04 = 4\ \%$
                 $3.15 = 315\ \%$
                 $84\% = 0.84$
                 $3\ \% = 0.03$
                 $60\% = 0.6$
                 $110\% = 1.1$
                 $\frac{1}{2}\% = 0.5\% = 0.005$

A **percent** can be converted to a **fraction** by placing it over 100 and reducing to simplest terms.

Example: Convert 0.056 to a fraction.

        Multiplying 0.056 by $\dfrac{1000}{1000}$ to get rid of the decimal point:

$$0.056 \times \frac{1000}{1000} = \frac{56}{1000} = \frac{7}{125}$$

Example: Find 23% of 1000.

$$= \frac{23}{100} \times \frac{1000}{1} = 23 \times 10 = 230$$

Example: Convert 6.25% to a decimal and to a fraction.

$$6.25\% = 0.0625 = 0.0625 \times \frac{10000}{10000} = \frac{625}{10000} = \frac{1}{16}$$

An example of a type of problem involving fractions is the conversion of recipes. For example, if a recipe serves 8 people and we want to make enough to serve only 4, we must determine how much of each ingredient to use. The conversion factor, the number we multiply each ingredient by, is:

$$\text{Conversion Factor} = \frac{\text{Number of Servings Needed}}{\text{Number of Servings in Recipe}}$$

Example: Consider the following recipe.

3 cups flour
½ tsp. baking powder
2/3 cups butter
2 cups sugar
2 eggs

If the above recipe serves 8, how much of each ingredient do we need to serve only 4 people?

First, determine the conversion factor.

$$\text{Conversion Factor} = \frac{4}{8} = \frac{1}{2}$$

Next, multiply each ingredient by the conversion factor.

3 x ½ =   1 ½ cups flour
½ x ½ =   ¼ tsp. baking powder
2/3 x ½ = 2/6 =   1/3 cups butter
2 x ½ =   1 cup sugar
2 x ½ =   1 egg

Skill 7.2 **Perform operations on integers, fractions, decimals, and percents**

Addition of whole numbers

Example: At the end of a day of shopping, a shopper had $24 remaining in his wallet. He spent $45 on various goods. How much money did the shopper have at the beginning of the day?

The total amount of money the shopper started with is the sum of the amount spent and the amount remaining at the end of the day.

$$\begin{array}{r} 24 \\ +\ 45 \\ \hline 69 \end{array}$$ → The original total was $69.

Example: A race took the winner 1 hr. 58 min. 12 sec. on the first half of the race and 2 hr. 9 min. 57 sec. on the second half of the race. How much time did the entire race take?

1 hr. 58 min. 12 sec.
+ 2 hr. 9 min. 57 sec.   Add these numbers
3 hr. 67 min. 69 sec.
    + 1 min–60 sec.   Change 60 seconds to 1
                               min.

3 hr. 68 min. 9 sec.
+ 1 hr.–60 min.   .   Change 60 minutes to 1 hr.
4 hr.   8 min. 9 sec. ←final answer

Subtraction of Whole Numbers

Example: At the end of his shift, a cashier has $96 in the cash register. At the beginning of his shift, he had $15. How much money did the cashier collect during his shift?

The total collected is the difference of the ending amount and the starting amount.

$$\begin{array}{r} 96 \\ -\ 15 \\ \hline 81 \end{array}$$ → The total collected was $81.

Multiplication of whole numbers

Multiplication is one of the four basic number operations. In simple terms, multiplication is the addition of a number to itself a certain number of times. For example, 4 multiplied by 3 is equal to 4 + 4 + 4 or 3 + 3 + 3 +3. Another way of conceptualizing multiplication is to think in terms of groups. For example, if we have 4 groups of 3 students, the total number of students is 4 multiplied by 3. We call the solution to a multiplication problem the product.

The basic algorithm for whole number multiplication begins with aligning the numbers by place value with the number containing more places on top.

$$\begin{array}{r} 172 \\ \times\ \ 43 \end{array}$$ → Note that we placed 172 on top because it has more places than 43 does.

Next, we multiply the ones place of the second number by each place value of the top number sequentially.

$$\begin{array}{r} (2) \\ 172 \\ \times\ \ 43 \\ \hline 516 \end{array}$$ → {3 x 2 = 6, 3 x 7 = 21, 3 x 1 = 3} Note that we had to carry a 2 to the hundreds column because 3 x 7 = 21. Note also that we add, not multiply, carried numbers to the product.

Next, we multiply the number in the tens place of the second number by each place value of the top number sequentially. Because we are multiplying by a number in the tens place, we place a zero at the end of this product.

$$\begin{array}{r} (2) \\ 172 \\ \times\ \ 43 \\ \hline 516 \\ 6880 \end{array}$$ → {4 x 2 = 8, 4 x 7 = 28, 4 x 1 = 4}

Finally, to determine the final product, we add the two partial products.

$$\begin{array}{r} 172 \\ \times\ \ 43 \\ \hline 516 \\ +\ 6880 \\ \hline 7396 \end{array}$$ → The product of 172 and 43 is 7396.

Example: A student buys 4 boxes of crayons. Each box contains 16 crayons. How many total crayons does the student have?

The total number of crayons is 16 x 4.

$$\begin{array}{r} 16 \\ \times\ 4 \\ \hline 64 \end{array}$$ → Total number of crayons equals 64.

Division of whole numbers

Division, the inverse of multiplication, is another of the four basic number operations. When we divide one number by another, we determine how many times we can multiply the divisor (number divided by) before we exceed the number we are dividing (dividend). For example, 8 divided by 2 equals 4 because we can multiply 2 four times to reach 8 (2 x 4 = 8 or 2 + 2 + 2 + 2 = 8). Using the grouping conceptualization we used with multiplication, we can divide 8 into 4 groups of 2 or 2 groups of 4. We call the answer to a division problem the quotient.

If the divisor does not divide evenly into the dividend, we express the leftover amount either as a remainder or as a fraction with the divisor as the denominator. For example, 9 divided by 2 equals 4 with a remainder of 1 or 4½.

The basic algorithm for division is long division. We start by representing the quotient as follows:

$14\overline{)293}$ → 14 is the divisor and 293 is the dividend.

This represents 293 ÷ 14.

Next, we divide the divisor into the dividend starting from the left.

$14\overline{)293}$ (with 2 above) → 14 divides into 29 two times with a remainder.

Next, we multiply the partial quotient by the divisor, subtract this value from the first digits of the dividend, and bring down the remaining dividend digits to complete the number.

$14\overline{)293}$, -28, 13 → 2 x 14 = 28, 29 – 28 = 1, and bringing down the 3 yields 13.

Finally, we divide again (the divisor into the remaining value) and repeat the preceding process. The number left after the subtraction represents the remainder.

$$
\begin{array}{r}
20 \\
14\overline{)293} \\
-28 \\
\hline
13 \\
-0 \\
\hline
13
\end{array}
$$

→ The final quotient is 20 with a remainder of 13. We can also represent this quotient as 20 13/14.

Example: Each box of apples contains 24 apples. How many boxes must a grocer purchase to supply a group of 252 people with one apple each?

The grocer needs 252 apples. Because he must buy apples in groups of 24, we divide 252 by 24 to determine how many boxes he needs to buy.

$$
\begin{array}{r}
10 \\
24\overline{)252} \\
-24 \\
\hline
12 \\
-0 \\
\hline
12
\end{array}
$$

→ The quotient is 10 with a remainder of 12.

Thus, the grocer needs 10 boxes plus 12 more apples. Therefore, the minimum number of boxes the grocer can purchase is 11.

Example: At his job, John gets paid $20 for every hour he works. If John made $940 in a week, how many hours did he work?

This is a division problem. To determine the number of hours John worked, we divide the total amount made ($940) by the hourly rate of pay ($20). Thus, the number of hours worked equals 940 divided by 20.

$$
\begin{array}{r}
47 \\
20\overline{)940} \\
-80 \\
\hline
140 \\
-140 \\
\hline
0
\end{array}
$$

→ 20 divides into 940, 47 times with no remainder.

John worked 47 hours.

Addition and Subtraction of Decimals

When adding and subtracting decimals, we align the numbers by place value as we do with whole numbers. After adding or subtracting each column, we bring the decimal down, placing it in the same location as in the numbers added or subtracted.

Example: Find the sum of 152.3 and 36.342.

$$
\begin{array}{r}
152.300 \\
+\ \ 36.342 \\
\hline
188.642
\end{array}
$$

Note that we placed two zeroes after the final place value in 152.3 to clarify the column addition.

Example: Find the difference of 152.3 and 36.342.

$$
\begin{array}{r}
2\ 9\ 10 \\
152.300 \\
-\ \ 36.342 \\
\hline
58
\end{array}
\qquad\longrightarrow\qquad
\begin{array}{r}
(4)11(12) \\
152.300 \\
-\ \ 36.342 \\
\hline
115.958
\end{array}
$$

Note how we borrowed to subtract from the zeroes in the hundredths and thousandths places of 152.300.

Multiplication of Decimals

When multiplying decimal numbers, we multiply exactly as with whole numbers and place the decimal in from the left the total number of decimal places contained in the two numbers multiplied. For example, when multiplying 1.5 and 2.35, we place the decimal in the product 3 places in from the left (3.525).

Example: Find the product of 3.52 and 4.1.

$$
\begin{array}{r}
3.52 \\
\times\ \ 4.1 \\
\hline
352 \\
+\ 14080 \\
\hline
14432
\end{array}
$$

Note that there are 3 total decimal places in the two numbers.

We place the decimal 3 places in from the left.

Thus, the final product is 14.432.

Example: A shopper has 5 one-dollar bills, 6 quarters, 3 nickels, and 4 pennies in his pocket. How much money does he have?

$$
\begin{array}{cccc}
& 3 & & \\
5 \times \$1.00 = \$5.00 & \$0.25 & \$0.05 & \$0.01 \\
& \underline{\times\ \ 6} & \underline{\times\ \ 3} & \underline{\times\ \ 4} \\
& \$1.50 & \$0.15 & \$0.04
\end{array}
$$

Note the placement of the decimals in the multiplication products. Thus, the total amount of money in the shopper's pocket is:

$$
\begin{array}{r}
\$5.00 \\
1.50 \\
0.15 \\
+\ \ 0.04 \\
\hline
\mathbf{\$6.69}
\end{array}
$$

Division of Decimals

When dividing decimal numbers, we first remove the decimal in the divisor by moving the decimal in the dividend the same number of spaces to the right. For example, when dividing 1.45 into 5.3 we convert the numbers to 145 and 530 and perform normal whole number division.

Example: Find the quotient of 5.3 divided by 1.45.
Convert to 145 and 530.

Divide.

$$
\begin{array}{r}
3 \\
145\overline{)530} \\
\underline{-435} \\
95
\end{array}
\qquad\longrightarrow\qquad
\begin{array}{r}
3.65 \\
145\overline{)530.00} \\
\underline{-435} \\
950 \\
\underline{-\ 870} \\
800
\end{array}
$$

→ Note that we insert the decimal to continue division.

Because one of the numbers divided contained one decimal place, we round the quotient to one decimal place. Thus, the final quotient is 3.7.

Operating with Percents

Example: 5 is what percent of 20?

This is the same as converting $\dfrac{5}{20}$ to % form.

$$\frac{5}{20} \times \frac{100}{1} = \frac{5}{1} \times \frac{5}{1} = 25\%$$

Example: There are 64 dogs in the kennel. 48 are collies. What percent are collies?

Restate the problem.   48 is what percent of 64?
Write an equation. $48 = n \times 64$
Solve. $\frac{48}{64} = n$

$n = \frac{3}{4} = 75\%$

75% of the dogs are collies.

Example: The auditorium was filled to 90% capacity. There were 558 seats occupied. What is the capacity of the auditorium?

Restate the problem.   90% of what number is 558?
Write an equation. $0.9n = 558$
Solve. $n = \frac{558}{.9}$
                           $n = 620$

The capacity of the auditorium is 620 people.

Example: A pair of shoes costs $42.00. Sales tax is 6%. What is the total cost of the shoes?

Restate the problem.   What is 6% of 42?
Write an equation. $n = 0.06 \times 42$
Solve. $n = 2.52$

Add the sales tax to the cost. $42.00 + $2.52 = $44.52

The total cost of the shoes, including sales tax, is $44.52.

Addition and subtraction of fractions

Key Points

1.   You need a common denominator in order to add and subtract reduced and improper fractions.

Example: $\dfrac{1}{3}+\dfrac{7}{3}=\dfrac{1+7}{3}=\dfrac{8}{3}=2\dfrac{2}{3}$

Example: $\dfrac{4}{12}+\dfrac{6}{12}-\dfrac{3}{12}=\dfrac{4+6-3}{12}=\dfrac{7}{12}$

2.   Adding an integer and a fraction of the <u>same</u> sign results directly in a mixed fraction.

Example: $2+\dfrac{2}{3}=2\dfrac{2}{3}$

Example: $^{-}2-\dfrac{3}{4}=^{-}2\dfrac{3}{4}$

3.   Adding an integer and a fraction with different signs involves the following steps.

-get a common denominator
-add or subtract as needed
-change to a mixed fraction if possible

Example: $2-\dfrac{1}{3}=\dfrac{2\times3-1}{3}=\dfrac{6-1}{3}=\dfrac{5}{3}=1\dfrac{2}{3}$

Example: Add $7\dfrac{3}{8}+5\dfrac{2}{7}$

Add the whole numbers; add the fractions and combine the two results:

$$7\dfrac{3}{8}+5\dfrac{2}{7}=(7+5)+(\dfrac{3}{8}+\dfrac{2}{7})$$
$$=12+\dfrac{(7\times3)+(8\times2)}{56}\quad\text{(LCM of 8 and 7)}$$
$$=12+\dfrac{21+16}{56}=12+\dfrac{37}{56}=12\dfrac{37}{56}$$

Example: Perform the operation.

$$\dfrac{2}{3}-\dfrac{5}{6}$$

We first find the LCM of 3 and 6, which is 6.

$$\frac{2\times 2}{3\times 2}-\frac{5}{6}\rightarrow\frac{4-5}{6}=\frac{^-1}{6}\qquad\text{(Using method A)}$$

Example: $^-7\frac{1}{4}+2\frac{7}{8}$

$$^-7\frac{1}{4}+2\frac{7}{8}=(^-7+2)+(\frac{^-1}{4}+\frac{7}{8})$$

$$=(^-5)+\frac{(^-2+7)}{8}=(^-5)+(\frac{5}{8})$$

$$=(^-5)+\frac{5}{8}=\frac{^-5\times 8}{1\times 8}+\frac{5}{8}=\frac{^-40+5}{8}$$

$$=\frac{^-35}{8}=^-4\frac{3}{8}$$

Divide 35 by 8 to get 4, remainder 3.

Caution: Common error would be

$$^-7\frac{1}{4}+2\frac{7}{8}=^-7\frac{2}{8}+2\frac{7}{8}=^-5\frac{9}{8}\qquad\text{Wrong.}$$

It is correct to add -7 and 2 to get -5, but adding $\frac{2}{8}+\frac{7}{8}=\frac{9}{8}$

is wrong. It should have been $\frac{^-2}{8}+\frac{7}{8}=\frac{5}{8}$. Then,

$$^-5+\frac{5}{8}=^-4\frac{3}{8}\quad\text{as before.}$$

Multiplication of fractions

Using the following example: $3\frac{1}{4}\times\frac{5}{6}$

1. Convert each number to an improper fraction.

$$3\frac{1}{4}=\frac{(12+1)}{4}=\frac{13}{4}\qquad\qquad\frac{5}{6}\text{ is already in reduced form.}$$

2. Reduce (cancel) common factors of the numerator and denominator if they exist.

$$\frac{13}{4} \times \frac{5}{6} \qquad \text{No common factors exist.}$$

3. Multiply the numerators by each other and the denominators by each other.

$$\frac{13}{4} \times \frac{5}{6} = \frac{65}{24}$$

4. If possible, reduce the fraction back to its lowest term.

$$\frac{65}{24} \qquad \text{Cannot be reduced further.}$$

5. Convert the improper fraction back to a mixed fraction by using long division.

$$\frac{65}{24} = 24\overline{)65} \qquad = 2\frac{17}{24}$$
$$\phantom{\frac{65}{24} = }\underline{48}$$
$$\phantom{\frac{65}{24} = 24)}17$$

Summary of sign changes for multiplication:

a. $(+) \times (+) = (+)$

b. $(-) \times (+) = (-)$

c. $(+) \times (-) = (-)$

d. $(-) \times (-) = (+)$

Example: $\quad 7\frac{1}{3} \times \frac{5}{11} = \frac{22}{3} \times \frac{5}{11} \qquad$ Reduce like terms (22 and 11)

$$= \frac{2}{3} \times \frac{5}{1} = \frac{10}{3} = 3\frac{1}{3}$$

Example: $\quad -6\frac{1}{4} \times \frac{5}{9} = \frac{^-25}{4} \times \frac{5}{9}$

$$= \frac{^-125}{36} = ^- 3\frac{17}{36}$$

Example: $\frac{^-1}{4} \times \frac{^-3}{7}$ Negative times a negative equals positive.

$$= \frac{1}{4} \times \frac{3}{7} = \frac{3}{28}$$

Division of fractions:

1. Change mixed fractions to improper fraction.

2. Change the division problem to a multiplication problem by using the reciprocal of the number after the division sign.

3. Find the sign of the final product.

4. Cancel if common factors exist between the numerator and the denominator.

5. Multiply the numerators together and the denominators together.

6. Change the improper fraction to a mixed number.

Example: $3\frac{1}{5} \div 2\frac{1}{4} = \frac{16}{5} \div \frac{9}{4}$

$$= \frac{16}{5} \times \frac{4}{9}$$ Reciprocal of $\frac{9}{4}$ is $\frac{4}{9}$.

$$= \frac{64}{45} = 1\frac{19}{45}$$

Example: $7\frac{3}{4} \div 11\frac{5}{8} = \frac{31}{4} \div \frac{93}{8}$

$$= \frac{31}{4} \times \frac{8}{93}$$ Reduce like terms.

$$= \frac{1}{1} \times \frac{2}{3} = \frac{2}{3}$$

Example:
$$\left(^-2\frac{1}{2}\right) \div 4\frac{1}{6} = \frac{^-5}{2} \div \frac{25}{6}$$

$$= \frac{^-5}{2} \times \frac{6}{25} \qquad \text{Reduce like terms.}$$

$$= \frac{^-1}{1} \times \frac{3}{5} = \frac{^-3}{5}$$

Example:
$$\left(^-5\frac{3}{8}\right) \div \left(\frac{^-7}{16}\right) = \frac{^-43}{8} \div \frac{^-7}{16}$$

$$= \frac{^-43}{8} \times \frac{^-16}{7} \qquad \text{Reduce like terms.}$$

$$= \frac{43}{1} \times \frac{2}{7} \qquad \text{Negative times a negative equals a positive.}$$

$$= \frac{86}{7} = 12\frac{2}{7}$$

Skill 7.3   Apply number properties (e.g., distributive, order of operations)

Properties are rules that apply for addition, subtraction, multiplication, or division of real numbers. These properties are:

Commutative: You can change the order of the terms or factors as follows:

For addition: $a + b = b + a$
For multiplication: $ab = ba$

Since addition is the inverse operation of subtraction and multiplication is the inverse operation of division, no separate laws are needed for subtraction and division.

Example: $5 + -8 = -8 + 5 = -3$

Example: $-2 \times 6 = 6 \times -2 = -12$

Associative: You can regroup the terms as you like.

For addition: $a + (b + c) = (a + b) + c$
For multiplication: $a(bc) = (ab)c$

This rule does not apply for division and subtraction.

Example: $(-2 + 7) + 5 = -2 + (7 + 5)$
$\qquad 5 + 5 = -2 + 12 = 10$

Example: $(3 \times -7) \times 5 = 3 \times (-7 \times 5)$
$\qquad -21 \times 5 = 3 \times -35 = -105$

Identity: Finding a number so that when added to a term results in that number (additive identity); finding a number such that when multiplied by a term results in that number (multiplicative identity).

For addition: $a + 0 = a$ (zero is additive identity)
For multiplication: $a \cdot 1 = a$ (one is multiplicative)

Example: $17 + 0 = 17$

Example: $-34 \times 1 = -34$
The product of any number and one is that number.

Inverse: Finding a number such that when added to the number it results in zero or when multiplied by the number results in 1.

For addition: $a + (-a) = 0$
For multiplication: $a \cdot (1/a) = 1$

$(-a)$ is the additive inverse of a; $1/a$, also called the reciprocal, is the multiplicative inverse of a.

Example: $25 + -25 = 0$

Example: $5 \times \frac{1}{5} = 1$ The product of any number and its reciprocal is one.

Distributive: This technique allows us to operate on terms within parentheses without first performing operations within the parentheses. This is especially helpful when terms within the parentheses cannot be combined.

$a (b + c) = ab + ac$

Example: $6 \times (-4 + 9) = (6 \times -4) + (6 \times 9)$
             $6 \times 5 = -24 + 54 = 30$

To multiply a sum by a number, multiply each addend by the number, then add the products.

The Order of Operations are to be followed when evaluating algebraic expressions. Follow these steps in order:

1. Simplify inside grouping characters such as parentheses, brackets, square root, fraction bar, etc.

2. Multiply out expressions with exponents.

3. Do multiplication or division, from left to right.

4. Do addition or subtraction, from left to right.

Example: $3^3 - 5(b + 2)$

$= 3^3 - 5b - 10$

$= 27 - 5b - 10 = 17 - 5b$

Example: $2 - 4 \times 2^3 - 2(4 - 2 \times 3)$

$= 2 - 4 \times 2^3 - 2(4 - 6) = 2 - 4 \times 2^3 - 2(^-2)$

$= 2 - 4 \times 2^3 + 4 = 2 - 4 \times 8 + 4$

$= 2 - 32 + 4 = 6 - 32 = ^- 26$

COMPETENCY 8.0   UNDERSTAND MEASUREMENT CONCEPTS AND PRINCIPLES OF GEOMETRY

Skill 8.1   Apply knowledge of measurement concepts (e.g., time, space, money)

Elapsed **time** problems are usually one of two types. One type of problem is the elapsed time between two times given in hours, minutes, and seconds. The other common type of problem is between two times given in months and years.

For any time of day past noon, change it into military time by adding 12 hours. For instance, 1:15 p.m. would be 13:15. Remember when you borrow a minute or an hour in a subtraction problem that you have borrowed 60 more seconds or minutes.

Example: Find the time from 11:34:22 a.m. until 3:28:40 p.m.

First, change 3:28:40 p.m. to   15:28:40 p.m.
Now subtract   − 11:34:22 a.m.
                                          :18

Borrow an hour and add 60 more minutes. Subtract
  14:88:40 p.m.
- 11:34:22 a.m.
   3:54:18 ↔ 3 hours, 54 minutes, 18 seconds

Example: A race took the winner 1 hr. 58 min. 12 sec. on the first half of the race and 2 hr. 9 min. 57 sec. on the second half of the race. How much time did the entire race take?

     1 hr. 58 min. 12 sec.
   + 2 hr. 9 min. 57 sec.   Add these numbers
     3 hr. 67 min. 69 sec
   +   1 min–60 sec.   Change 60 seconds to 1 min.
     3 hr. 68 min.   9 sec.
   + 1 hr.–60 min.   .   Change 60 minutes to 1 hr.
     4 hr.   8 min.   9 sec. ← final answer

Example: It takes Cynthia 45 minutes to get ready each morning. How many hours does she spend getting ready each week?

45 minutes X 7 days = 315 minutes

$\dfrac{315 \text{ minutes}}{60 \text{ minutes in an hour}}$ =   5.25 hours

Money

Example: Janet goes into a store to purchase a CD on sale for $13.95. While shopping, she sees two pairs of shoes, prices $19.95 and $14.50. She only has $50. Can she purchase everything?

Solve by rounding:

$19.95→$20.00
$14.50→$15.00
$13.95→$14.00
　　　　$49.00   Yes, she can purchase the CD and the shoes.

Weight

Example: The weight limit of a playground merry-go-round is 1000 pounds.
There are 11 children on the merry-go-round.
3 children weigh 100 pounds.
6 children weigh 75 pounds.
2 children weigh 60 pounds.

George weighs 80 pounds. Can he get on the merry-go-round?

3(100) + 6(75) + 2(60)
= 300 + 450 + 120
= 870
1000 − 870
= 130

Since 80 is less than 130, George can get on the merry-go-round.

Skill 8.2 **Select and convert units within and between standard and metric measurement systems**

<u>Measurements of length (English system)</u>

12 inches (in)	=	1 foot (ft)
3 feet (ft)	=	1 yard (yd)
1760 yards (yd)	=	1 mile (mi)

<u>Measurements of length (Metric system)</u>

kilometer (km)	=	1000 meters (m)
hectometer (hm)	=	100 meters (m)
decameter (dam)	=	10 meters (m)
meter (m)	=	1 meter (m)
decimeter (dm)	=	1/10 meter (m)
centimeter (cm)	=	1/100 meter (m)
millimeter (mm)	=	1/1000 meter (m)

<u>Conversion of length from English to Metric</u>

1 inch	=	2.54 centimeters
1 foot	≈	30 centimeters
1 yard	≈	0.9 meters
1 mile	≈	1.6 kilometers

<u>Measurements of weight (English system)</u>

28 grams (g)	=	1 ounce (oz)
16 ounces (oz)	=	1 pound (lb)
2000 pounds (lb)	=	1 ton (t)(short ton)
1.1 ton (t)	=	1 ton (t)

<u>Measurements of weight (Metric system)</u>

kilogram (kg)	=	1000 grams (g)
gram (g)	=	1 gram (g)
milligram (mg)	=	1/1000 gram (g)

<u>Conversion of weight from English to metric</u>

1 ounce	≈	28 grams
1 pound	≈	0.45 kilogram
	≈	454 grams

Measurement of volume (English system)

8 fluid ounces (oz)	=	1 cup (c)
2 cups (c)	=	1 pint (pt)
2 pints (pt)	=	1 quart (qt)
4 quarts (qt)	=	1 gallon (gal)

Measurement of volume (Metric system)

kiloliter (kl)	=	1000 liters (l)
liter (l)	=	1 liter (l)
milliliter (ml)	=	1/1000 liters (ml)

Conversion of volume from English to metric

1 teaspoon (tsp)	≈	5 milliliters
1 fluid ounce	≈	15 milliliters
1 cup	≈	0.24 liters
1 pint	≈	0.47 liters
1 quart	≈	0.95 liters
1 gallon	≈	3.8 liters

Measurement of time

1 second	=	
1 minute	=	60 seconds
1 hour	=	60 minutes
1 day	=	24 hours
1 week	=	7 days
1 year	=	365 days
1 century	=	100 years

Note: (') represents feet and (") represents inches.

Skill 8.3   Apply knowledge of the language of geometry (e.g., points, lines, angles, distance) in various situations

A point, a line, and a plane are actually undefined terms since we cannot give a satisfactory definition using simple defined terms. However, their properties and characteristics give a clear understanding of what they are.

A **point** indicates place or position. It has no length, width, or thickness.

point A

A **line** is considered a set of points. Lines may be straight or curved, but the term line commonly denotes a straight line. Lines extend indefinitely.

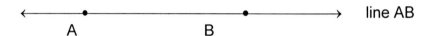
line AB

A **plane** is a set of points composing a flat surface. A plane also has no boundaries.

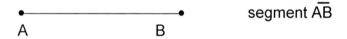
plane A

A **line segment** has two endpoints.

segment $\overline{AB}$

A **ray** has exactly one endpoint. It extends indefinitely in one direction.

ray $\overrightarrow{AB}$

An **angle** is formed by the intersection of two rays.

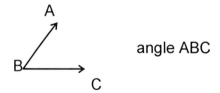
angle ABC

Angles are measured in degrees. $1° = \frac{1}{360}$ of a circle.

A **right angle** measures 90°.

An **acute angle** measures more than 0° and less than 90°.

An **obtuse angle** measures more than 90° and less than 180°.

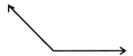

A **straight angle** measures 180°.

A **reflexive angle** measures more than 180° and less than 360°.

An infinite number of lines can be drawn through any point.

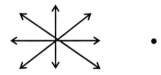

Exactly one line can be drawn through two points.

Intersecting lines share a common point and intersecting planes share a common set of points or line.

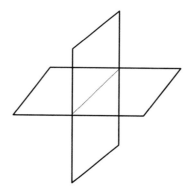

Skew lines do not intersect and do not lie on the same plane.

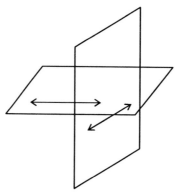

Perpendicular lines or planes form a 90-degree angle to each other. Perpendicular lines have slopes that are negative reciprocals.

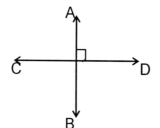

Line AB is perpendicular to line CD.

AB ⊥ CD

Parallel lines or planes do not intersect. Two parallel lines will have the same slope and are everywhere equidistant.

Line AB is parallel to line CD.

AB ∥ CD

Skill 8.4   Analyze fundamental properties of basic geometric shapes

Polygons, simple closed **two-dimensional figures** composed of line segments, are named according to the number of sides they have.

A **quadrilateral** is a polygon with four sides.
The sum of the measures of the angles of a quadrilateral is 360°.

A **trapezoid** is a quadrilateral with exactly <u>one</u> pair of parallel sides.

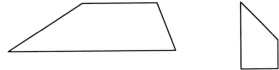

In an **isosceles trapezoid**, the non-parallel sides are congruent.

A **parallelogram** is a quadrilateral with <u>two</u> pairs of parallel sides.

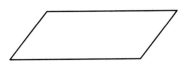

In a parallelogram:
The diagonals bisect each other.
Each diagonal divides the parallelogram into two congruent triangles.
Both pairs of opposite sides are congruent.
Both pairs of opposite angles are congruent.
Two adjacent angles are supplementary.

A **rectangle** is a parallelogram with a right angle.

A **rhombus** is a parallelogram with all sides equal in length.

A **square** is a rectangle with all sides equal in length.

Example: True or false?
            All squares are rhombuses.   True
            All parallelograms are rectangles.   False—<u>some</u>
                                                          parallelograms are
                                                          rectangles

            All rectangles are parallelograms.   True
            Some rhombuses are squares.   True
            Some rectangles are trapezoids.   False—only <u>one</u> pair of
                                                          parallel sides

            All quadrilaterals are parallelograms.   False—some
                                                          quadrilaterals are
                                                          parallelograms

            Some squares are rectangles.   False—all squares are
                                                          rectangles

            Some parallelograms are rhombuses.   True

A **triangle** is a polygon with three sides.

Triangles can be classified by the types of angles or the lengths of their sides.

An **acute** triangle has exactly three *acute* angles.
A **right** triangle has one *right* angle.
An **obtuse** triangle has one *obtuse* angle.

        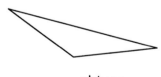

acute   right   obtuse

All *three* sides of an **equilateral** triangle are the same length.
Two sides of an **isosceles** triangle are the same length.
None of the sides of a **scalene** triangle is the same length.

        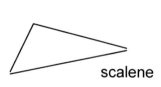

equilateral   isosceles   scalene

Example: Can a triangle have two right angles?
No. A right angle measures 90°; therefore, the sum of two right angles would be 180° and there could not be a third angle.

Example: Can a triangle have two obtuse angles?
No. Since an obtuse angle measures more than 90°, the sum of two obtuse angles would be greater than 180°.

A **cylinder** has two congruent circular bases that are parallel.

A **sphere** is a space figure having all its points the same distance from the center.

A **cone** is a space figure having a circular base and a single vertex.

A **pyramid** is a space figure with a square base and four triangle-shaped sides.

A **tetrahedron** is a 4-sided space triangle. Each face is a triangle.

A **prism** is a space figure with two congruent, parallel bases that are polygons.

Skill 8.5   Determine the length, perimeter, area, and volume of geometric shapes or figures

The **perimeter** of any polygon is the sum of the lengths of the sides.

The **area** of a polygon is the number of square units covered by the figure.

FIGURE	AREA FORMULA	PERIMETER FORMULA
Rectangle	LW	$2(L+W)$
Triangle	$\frac{1}{2}bh$	$a+b+c$
Parallelogram	bh	sum of lengths of sides
Trapezoid	$\frac{1}{2}h(a+b)$	sum of lengths of sides

Example: A farmer has a piece of land shaped as shown below. He wishes to fence this land at an estimated cost of $25 per linear foot. What is the total cost of fencing this property to the nearest foot?

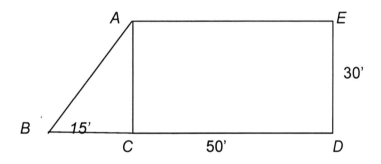

From the right triangle ABC, AC = 30 and BC = 15.

Since $(AB) = (AC)^2 + (BC)^2$
$(AB) = (30)^2 + (15)^2$

So $\sqrt{(AB)^2} = AB = \sqrt{1125} = 33.5410$ feet

To the nearest foot AB = 34 feet.

Perimeter of the piece of land = $AB + BC + CD + DE + EA$

= 34 + 15 + 50 + 30 + 50 = 179 feet

cost of fencing = $25 x 179 = $4, 475.00

Area

Area is the space that a figure occupies.

Example: What will be the cost of carpeting a rectangular office that measures 12 feet by 15 feet if the carpet costs $12.50 per square yard?

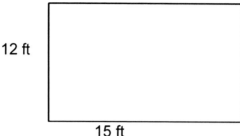

12 ft

15 ft

The problem is asking you to determine the area of the office. The area of a rectangle is *length x width = A*
Substitute the given values in the equation $A = lw$

$A = (12 \text{ ft.}) (15 \text{ ft.})$

$A = 180 \text{ ft.}$

The problem asked you to determine the cost of carpet at $12.50 per square yard.

First, you need to convert 180 ft.^{2} into yards^2.

1 yd. = 3 ft.
(1 yard)(1 yard) = (3 feet)(3 feet)
$1 \text{ yd}^2 = 9 \text{ ft}^2$

Hence, $\dfrac{180 \text{ ft}^2}{1} = \dfrac{1 \text{ yd}^2}{9 \text{ ft}^2} = \dfrac{20}{1} = 20 \text{ yd}^2$

The carpet costs $12.50 per square yard; thus, the cost of carpeting the office described is $12.50 x 20 = $250.00.

Example: Find the area of a parallelogram whose base is 6.5 cm and the height of the altitude to that base is 3.7 cm.

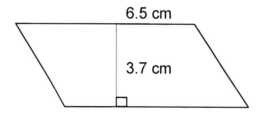

6.5 cm

3.7 cm

$$A_{parallelogram} = bh$$

$$= (3.7)(6.5)$$
$$= 24.05 \text{ cm}^2$$

Example: Find the area of this triangle.

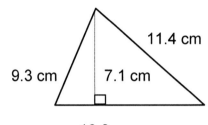

$$A_{triangle} = \frac{1}{2}bh$$
$$= 0.5 (16.8) (7.1)$$
$$= 59.64 \text{ cm}^2$$

Example: Find the area of this trapezoid.

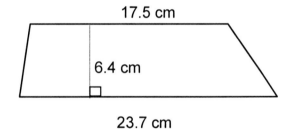

The area of a trapezoid equals one-half the sum of the bases times the altitude.

$$A_{trapezoid} = \frac{1}{2}h(b_1 + b_2)$$
$$= 0.5 (6.4) (17.5 + 23.7)$$
$$= 131.84 \text{ cm}^2$$

The distance around a circle is the **circumference**. The ratio of the circumference to the diameter is represented by the Greek letter pi.

$$\Pi \sim 3.14 \sim \frac{22}{7}.$$

The circumference of a circle is found by the formula $C = 2\Pi r$ or $C = \Pi d$ where r is the radius of the circle and d is the diameter.

The **area** of a circle is found by the formula $A = \Pi r^2$.

Example: Find the circumference and area of a circle whose radius is 7 meters.

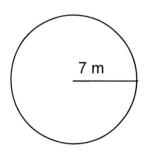

7 m

C = 2Πr   A = Πr²
= 2(3.14)(7)   = 3.14(7)(7)
= 43.96 m   = 153.86 m²

Volume and **Surface area** are computed using the following formulas:

FIGURE	VOLUME	TOTAL SURFACE AREA
Right Cylinder	$\pi r^2 h$	$2\pi rh + 2\pi r^2$
Right Cone	$\dfrac{\pi r^2 h}{3}$	$\pi r\sqrt{r^2 + h^2} + \pi r^2$
Sphere	$\dfrac{4}{3}\pi r^3$	$4\pi r^2$
Rectangular Solid	LWH	$2LW + 2WH + 2LH$

FIGURE	LATERAL AREA	TOTAL AREA	VOLUME
Regular Pyramid	1/2Pl	1/2Pl+B	1/3Bh

P = Perimeter
h = height
B = Area of Base
l = slant height

Example: What is the volume of a shoebox with a length of 35 cm, a width of 20 cm, and a height of 15 cm?

Volume of a rectangular solid
= Length x Width x Height
= 35 x 20 x 15
= 10500 cm³

Example: A water company is trying to decide whether to use traditional cylindrical paper cups or to offer conical paper cups since both cost the same. The traditional cups are 8 cm wide and 14 cm high. The conical cups are 12 cm wide and 19 cm high. The company will use the cup that holds the most water.

Draw and label a sketch of each.

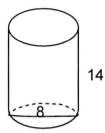 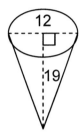

$V = \pi r^2 h$	$V = \dfrac{\pi r^2 h}{3}$	1. write formula
$V = \pi (4)^2 (14)$	$V = \dfrac{1}{3} \pi (6)^2 (19)$	2. substitute
$V = 703.717$ cm^3	$V = 716.283$ cm^3	3. solve

The choice should be the conical cup since its volume is more.

Example: How much material is needed to make a basketball that has a diameter of 15 inches? How much air is needed to fill the basketball?

Draw and label a sketch:

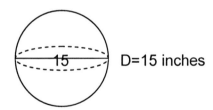 D=15 inches

Total surface area　　　Volume

$TSA = 4\pi r^2$	$V = \dfrac{4}{3} \pi r^3$	1. write formula
$= 4\pi (7.5)^2$	$= \dfrac{4}{3} \pi (7.5)^3$	2. substitute
$= 706.858$ in^2	$= 1767.1459$ in^3	3. solve

COMPETENCY 9.0   UNDERSTAND STATISTICAL CONCEPTS AND DATA
ANALYSIS AND INTERPRETATION

Skill 9.1   Interpret information presented in line graphs, scatter plots,
pictographs, bar graphs, histograms, tables, and pie graphs

To make a **bar graph** or a **pictograph**, determine the scale to be used for the
graph. Then determine the length of each bar on the graph or determine the
number of pictures needed to represent each item of information. Be sure to
include an explanation of the scale in the legend.

Example: A class had the following grades:
4 A's, 9 B's, 8 C's, 1 D, 3 F's.
Graph these on a pictograph and a bar graph.

Pictograph

Grade	Number of Students
A	😊😊😊😊
B	😊😊😊😊😊😊😊😊😊
C	😊😊😊😊😊😊😊😊
D	😊
F	😊😊😊

Bar graph

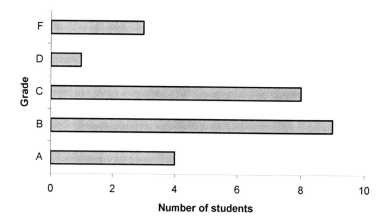

To make a **line graph**, determine appropriate scales for both the vertical and horizontal axes (based on the information to be graphed). Describe what each axis represents and mark the scale periodically on each axis. Graph the individual points of the graph and connect the points on the graph from left to right.

Example: Graph the following information using a line graph.

The number of National Merit finalists/school year

	90–91	91–92	92–93	93–94	94–95	95–96
Central	3	5	1	4	6	8
Wilson	4	2	3	2	3	2

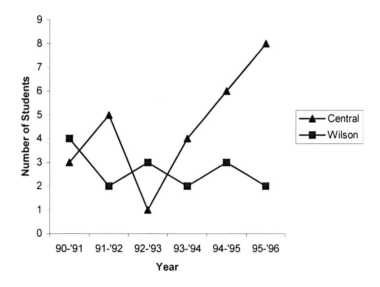

To make a **circle graph**, total all the information that is to be included on the graph. Determine the central angle to be used for each sector of the graph using the following formula:

$$\frac{\text{information}}{\text{total information}} \times 360° = \text{degrees in central} \angle$$

Lay out the central angles to these sizes, label each section, and include its percent.

Example: Graph this information on a circle graph:

Monthly expenses:

Rent, $400
Food, $150
Utilities, $75
Clothes, $75
Church, $100
Misc., $200

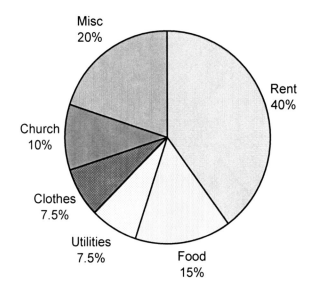

Scatter plots compare two characteristics of the same group of things or people and usually consist of a large body of data. They show how much one variable affects another. The relationship between the two variables is their **correlation**. The closer the data points come to making a straight line when plotted, the closer the correlation.

Stem and leaf plots are visually similar to line plots. The **stems** are the digits in the greatest place value of the data values, and the **leaves** are the digits in the next greatest place value. Stem and leaf plots are best suited for small sets of data and are especially useful for comparing two sets of data. The following is an example using test scores:

4	9
5	4 9
6	1 2 3 4 6 7 8 8
7	0 3 4 6 6 6 7 7 7 8 8 8 8
8	3 5 5 7 8
9	0 0 3 4 5
10	0 0

Histograms are used to summarize information from large sets of data that can be naturally grouped into intervals. The vertical axis indicates **frequency** (the number of times any particular data value occurs), and the horizontal axis indicates data values or ranges of data values. The number of data values in any interval is the **frequency of the interval**.

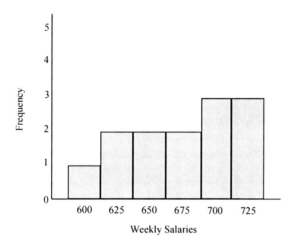

A relationship between two quantities can be shown using a table, graph, or rule. In this example, the rule y= 9x describes the relationship between the total amount earned, y, and the total amount of $9 sunglasses sold, x.

A table using this data would appear as:

number of sunglasses sold	1	5	10	15
total dollars earned	9	45	90	135

Each *(x, y)* relationship between a pair of values is called the coordinate pair and can be plotted on a graph. The coordinate pairs (1,9), (5,45), (10,90), and (15,135), are plotted on the graph below.

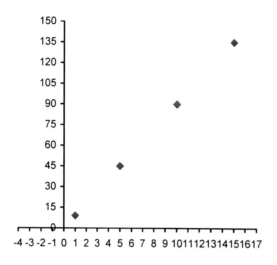

The graph shows a linear relationship. A linear relationship is one in which two quantities are proportional to each other. Doubling *x* also doubles *y*. On a graph, a straight line depicts a linear relationship.

The function or relationship between two quantities may be analyzed to determine how one quantity depends on the other. For example, the function below shows a relationship between y and x:

y = 2x+1

The relationship between two or more variables can be analyzed using a table, graph, written description, or symbolic rule. The function, y = 2x + 1, is written as a symbolic rule. The same relationship is also shown in the table below:

x	0	2	3	6	9
y	1	5	7	13	19

A relationship could be written in words by saying the value of y is equal to two times the value of x, plus one. This relationship could be shown on a graph by plotting given points such as the ones shown in the table above.

Another way to describe a function is as a process in which one or more numbers are input into an imaginary machine that produces another number as the output. If 5 is input, x, into a machine with a process of x + 1, the output, y, will equal 6.

In real situations, relationships can be described mathematically. The function, $y = x + 1$, can be used to describe the idea that people age one year on their birthday. To describe the relationship in which a person's monthly medical costs are six times a person's age, we could write $y = 6x$. The monthly cost of medical care could be predicted using this function. A 20-year-old person would spend $120 per month ($120 = 20 * 6$). An 80 year-old person would spend $480 per month ($480 = 80 * 6$). Therefore, one could analyze the relationship to say, "as you get older, medical costs increase $6.00 each year."

Skill 9.2   Determine the theoretical probability of simple events

In probability, the **sample space** is a list of all possible outcomes of an experiment. For example, the sample space of tossing two coins is the set {HH, HT, TT, TH}, the sample space of rolling a six-sided die is the set {1, 2, 3, 4, 5, 6}, and the sample space of measuring the height of students in a class is the set of all real numbers {R}. **Probability** measures the chances of an event occurring. The probability of an event that *must* occur, a certain event, is **one**. When no outcome is favorable, the probability of an impossible event is **zero.**

$$P(event) = \frac{number\ of\ favorable\ outcomes}{number\ of\ possible\ outcomes}$$

Example: Given one die with faces numbered 1–6, the probability of tossing an even number on one throw of the die is 3/6 or ½ since there are three favorable outcomes (even faces) and a total of six possible outcomes (faces).

Example: If a fair die is rolled.

a) Find the probability of rolling an even number.
b) Find the probability of rolling a number less than three.

a) The sample space is

S = {1, 2, 3, 4, 5, 6} and the event representing even numbers is

E = {2, 4, 6}

Hence, the probability of rolling an even number is

$$p(E) = \frac{n(E)}{n(S)} = \frac{3}{6} = \frac{1}{2} \text{ or } 0.5$$

b) The event of rolling a number less than three is represented by

A = {1, 2}

Hence, the probability of rolling a number less than three is

$$p(A) = \frac{n(A)}{n(S)} = \frac{2}{6} = \frac{1}{3} \text{ or } 0.33$$

Example: A class has thirty students. Out of the thirty students, twenty-four are males. Assuming all the students have the same chance of being selected, find the probability of selecting a female. (Only one person is selected.)

The number of females in the class is

$$30 - 24 = 6$$

Hence, the probability of selecting a female is

$$p(female) = \frac{6}{30} = \frac{1}{5} \text{ or } 0.2$$

If A and B are **independent** events, then the outcome of event A does not affect the outcome of event B or vice versa. The multiplication rule is used to find joint probability.

$$P(A \text{ and } B) = P(A) \times P(B)$$

Example: The probability that a patient is allergic to aspirin is 0.30. If the probability of a patient having a window in his/her room is 0.40, find the probability that the patient is allergic to aspirin and has a window in his/her room.

Defining the events: A = The patient being allergic to aspirin.
                                 B = The patient has a window in his/her room.

Events A and B are independent, hence
$p(A \text{ and } B) = p(A) \cdot p(B)$
$= (0.30)(0.40)$
$= 0.12 \text{ or } 12\%$

Example: Given a jar containing 10 marbles—3 red, 5 black, and 2 white— what is the probability of drawing a red marble and then a white marble if the marble is returned to the jar after choosing?
3/10 X 2/10 = 6/100 = 3/50

When the outcome of the first event affects the outcome of the second event, the events are **dependent.** Any two events that are not independent are dependent. This is also known as conditional probability.

Probability of (A and B) = P(A) × P(B given A)

Example: Two cards are drawn from a deck of 52 cards without replacement; that is, the first card is not returned to the deck before the second card is drawn. What is the probability of drawing a diamond?

A = drawing a diamond first
B = drawing a diamond second
P(A) = drawing a diamond first
P(B) = drawing a diamond second

P(A) = 13/52 = ¼   P(B) = 12/52 = 4/17
(PA+B) = ¼ X 4/17 = 1/17

Example: A class of ten students has six males and four females. If two students are selected to represent the class, find the probability that

a) the first is a male and the second is a female
b) the first is a female and the second is a male
c) both are females
d) both are males

Defining the events: F = a female is selected to represent the class.
M = a male is selected to represent the class.
F/M = a female is selected after a male has been selected.
M/F = a male is selected after a female has been selected.

a)   Since F and M are dependent events, it follows that
P(M and F) = P(M) · P(F/M)
$$= \frac{6}{10} X \frac{4}{9} = \frac{3}{5} X \frac{4}{9} = \frac{12}{45}$$

$P(F/M) = \dfrac{4}{9}$ instead of $\dfrac{4}{10}$ since the selection of a male first changed the Sample Space from ten to nine students.

b) $P(F \text{ and } M) = P(F) \cdot P(M/F)$

$= \dfrac{4}{10} \times \dfrac{6}{9} = \dfrac{2}{5} \times \dfrac{2}{3} = \dfrac{4}{15}$

c) $P(F \text{ and } F) = p(F) \cdot p(F/F)$

$= \dfrac{4}{10} \times \dfrac{3}{9} = \dfrac{2}{5} \times \dfrac{1}{3} = \dfrac{2}{15}$

d) $P(\text{both are males}) = p(M \text{ and } M)$

$= \dfrac{6}{10} \times \dfrac{5}{9} = \dfrac{30}{90} = \dfrac{1}{3}$

Skill 9.3 **Demonstrate knowledge of measures of central tendency (e.g., mean, median) and variability (e.g., range, deviation from the mean)**

The arithmetic **mean** (or average) of a set of numbers is the *sum* of the numbers given *divided* by the number of items being averaged.

Example: Find the mean. Round to the nearest tenth.

24.6, 57.3, 44.1, 39.8, 64.5
The sum is 230.3 ÷ 5 = 46.06, rounded to 46.1

The **median** of a set is the middle number. To calculate the median, the terms must be arranged in order. If there is an even number of terms, the median is the mean of the two middle terms.

Example: Find the median.

12, 14, 27, 3, 13, 7, 17, 12, 22, 6, 16

Rearrange the terms.

3, 6, 7, 12, 12, 13, 14, 16, 17, 22, 27

Since there are eleven numbers, the middle would be the sixth number or 13.

The **mode** of a set of numbers is the number that occurs with the greatest frequency. A set can have no mode if each term appears exactly one time. Similarly, there can also be more than one mode.

Example: Find the mode.

26, 15, 37, **26,** 35, **26,** 15

15 appears twice, but 26 appears 3 times, therefore, the mode is 26.

The **range** is the difference between the highest and lowest value of data items.

Example: Given the ungrouped data below, calculate the mean and range.

| 15 | 22 | 28 | 25 | 34 | 38 |
| 18 | 25 | 30 | 33 | 19 | 23 |

Mean ($\overline{X}$) = 25.8333333
Range: $38 - 15 = 23$

Percentiles divide data into 100 equal parts. A person whose score falls in the 65th percentile has outperformed 65 percent of all those who took the test. This does not mean that the score was 65 out of 100 nor does it mean that 65 percent of the questions answered were correct. It means that the grade was higher than 65 percent of all those who took the test.

Stanine, "standard nine," scores combine the understandability of percentages with the properties of the normal curve of probability. Stanines divide the bell curve into nine sections, the largest of which stretches from the 40th to the 60th percentile and is the "Fifth Stanine" (the average of taking into account error possibilities).

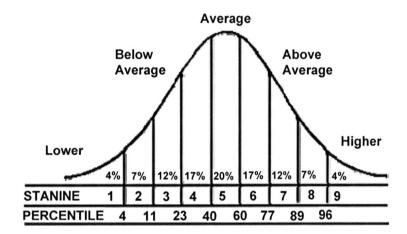

Quartiles divide the data into four parts. First, find the median of the data set (Q2), then find the median of the upper (Q3) and lower (Q1) halves of the data set. If there are an odd number of values in the data set, include the median value in both halves when finding quartile values. For example, given the data set {1, 4, 9, 16, 25, 36, 49, 64, 81}, first find the median value, which is 25. This is the second quartile. Since there are an odd number of values in the data set (9), we include the median in both halves.

To find the quartile values, we much find the medians of {1, 4, 9, 16, 25} and {25, 36, 49, 64, 81}. Since each of these subsets has an odd number of elements (5), we use the middle value. Thus, the first quartile value is 9 and the third quartile value is 49. If the data set has an even number of elements, average the middle two values. The quartile values are always either one of the data points, or exactly halfway between two data points.

Example: Given the following set of data, find the percentile of the score 104.

70, 72, 82, 83, 84, 87, 100, 104, 108, 109, 110, 115

Find the percentage of scores below 104.

7/12 of the scores are less than 104. This is 58.333%; therefore, the score of 104 is in the 58th percentile.

Example: Find the first, second and third quartile for the data listed.

6, 7, 8, 9, 10, 12, 13, 14, 15, 16, 18, 23, 24, 25, 27, 29, 30, 33, 34, 37

Quartile 1: The 1st Quartile is the median of the lower half of the data set, which is 11.

Quartile 2: The median of the data set is the 2nd Quartile, which is 17.

Quartile 3: The 3rd Quartile is the median of the upper half of the data set, which is 28.

Skill 9.4 Demonstrate knowledge of the use of statistical concepts in real-world situations

A **trend** line on a line graph shows the correlation between two sets of data. A trend may show positive correlation (both sets of data get bigger together), negative correlation (one set of data gets bigger while the other gets smaller), or no correlation.

An **inference** is a statement that is derived from reasoning. When reading a graph, inferences help with interpretation of the data that is being presented. From this information, a **conclusion** and even **predictions** about what the data actually means is possible.

Example: Katherine and Tom were both doing poorly in math class. Their teacher had a conference with each of them in November. The following graph shows their math test scores during the school year.

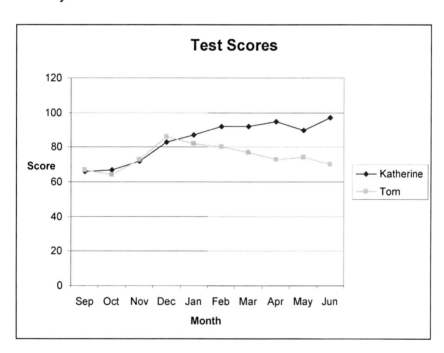

What kind of trend does this graph show?

This graph shows that there is a positive trend in Katherine's test scores and a negative trend in Tom's test scores.

What inferences can you make from this graph?

We can infer that Katherine's test scores rose steadily after November. Tom's test scores spiked in December but then began to fall again and became negatively trended.

What conclusion can you draw based upon this graph?

We can conclude that Katherine took her teacher's meeting seriously and began to study in order to do better on the exams. It seems as though Tom tried harder for a bit, but his test scores eventually slipped back down to the level where he began.

COMPETENCY 10.0 UNDERSTAND PROBLEM-SOLVING PRINCIPLES AND TECHNIQUES

Skill 10.1 Identify missing terms in numerical and graphical patterns

Example: A fish is 30 inches long. The head is as long as the tail. If the head was twice as long and the tail was its present length, the body would be 18 inches long. How long is the body?

Partial solution: Let x represent the head.

$$2x + x + 18 = 30$$
$$3x = 12$$
$$x = 4$$

We now create an equation to solve for the body of the fish with y representing the body.

$$x + x + y = 30$$
$$2x + y = 30$$
Substitute 4 for x.
$$2(4) + y = 30$$
$$8 + y = 30$$
$$y = 22$$

In this example, we are able to substitute the partial solution to solve for the variable in the problem's actual question.

Example: How many squares must be added to a 10-by-10 square to create an 11-by-11 square?

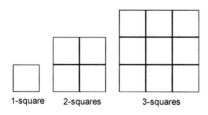

1-square   2-squares   3-squares

Partial solution: We determine that a 3-by-3 square has five more squares than a 2-by-2 square, which has three more squares than one square.

By examining the pattern, we see that we can answer the question by adding the dimension of the previous square (in this case, 10) to the dimension of the current square (in this case, 11) to answer the question. Twenty-one squares must be added to a 10-by-10 square to create an 11-by-11 square.

Skill 10.2   Solve problems and drawing conclusions using deductive reasoning

A simple statement represents a simple idea, that can be described either as *true* or *false*, but not both. A small letter of the alphabet represents a simple statement.

Example: "Today is Monday." This is a simple statement since it can be determined that this statement is either true or false. We can write *p* = "Today is Monday."

Example: "John, please be quiet." This is not considered a simple statement in our study of logic, since we cannot assign a truth value to it.

Simple statements joined by **connectives** (*and, or, not, if then*, and *if and only if*) result in compound statements. Note that compound statements can also be formed using *but, however*, or *nevertheless*. A compound statement can be assigned a truth value.

Conditional statements are frequently written in *if-then* form. The *if* clause of the conditional is known as the **hypothesis**, and the *then* clause is called the **conclusion**. In a proof, the hypothesis is the information that is assumed true, while the conclusion is what is to be proven true. A conditional is considered to be of the form: **If *p*, then *q*,** where *p* is the hypothesis and *q* is the conclusion.

$p \rightarrow q$ is read, "If *p*, then *q*."
~ (statement) is read, "It is not true that (statement)."

Quantifiers are words describing a quantity under discussion. These include words such as *all, none* (or *no*), and *some*.

Negation of a Statement—If a statement is true, then its negation must be false (and vice versa).

A Summary of Negation Rules:

statement	negation
(1) *q*	(1) <u>not</u> *q*
(2) <u>not</u> *q*	(2) *q*
(3) π <u>and</u> *s*	(3) (not π) <u>or</u> (not *s*)
(4) π <u>or</u> *s*	(4) (not π) <u>and</u> (not *s*)
(5) if *p*, then *q*	(5) (*p*) <u>and</u> (not *q*)

Example: Select the statement that is the negation of "some winter nights are not cold."

A. All winter nights are not cold.
B. Some winter nights are cold.
C. All winter nights are cold.
D. None of the winter nights is cold.

Negation of *some are* is *none is*. Therefore, the negation statement is "None of the winter nights is cold." Therefore, the answer is D.

Example: Select the statement that is the negation of "If it rains, then the beach party will not be held."

A. If it does not rain, then the beach party will be held.
B. If the beach party is held, then it will not rain.
C. It does not rain and the beach party will be held.
D. It rains and the beach party will be held.

Negation of "If p, then q" is "p and (not q)." Therefore, the negation of the given statement is "It rains and the beach party will be held." So select D.

Example: Select the negation of the statement "If they get elected, then all politicians go back on election promises."

A. If they get elected, then many politicians go back on election promises.
B. They get elected and some politicians go back on election promises.
C. If they do not get elected, some politicians do not go back on election promises.
D. None of the above statements is the negation of the given statement.

Identify the key words of "if...then" and "all...go back". The negation of the given statement is "They get elected and none of the politicians goes back on election promises." So select response D, since statements A, B, and C are not the negations.

Example: Select the statement that is the negation of "the sun is shining bright <u>and</u> I feel great."
A. If the sun is not shining bright, I do not feel great.
B. The sun is not shining bright and I do not feel great.
C. The sun is not shining bring or I do not feel great.
D. The sun is shining bright and I do not feel great.

The negation of "*r* and *s*" is "(not *r*) or (not *s*)." So the negation of the given statement is "The sun is <u>not</u> shining bright <u>or</u> I do not feel great." We select response C.

Conditional statements can be diagrammed using a **Venn diagram**. A diagram can be drawn with one circle inside another circle. The inner circle represents the hypothesis. The outer circle represents the conclusion. If the hypothesis is taken to be true, then you are located inside the inner circle. If you are located in the inner circle then you are also inside the outer circle, so that proves the conclusion is true.

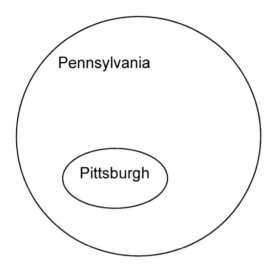

Example: If an angle has a measure of 90 degrees, then it is a right angle.

In this statement, "an angle has a measure of 90 degrees," is the hypothesis. In this statement, "it is a right angle" is the conclusion.

Example: If you are in Pittsburgh, then you are in Pennsylvania.

In this statement, "you are in Pittsburgh" is the hypothesis.
In this statement, "you are in Pennsylvania" is the conclusion.

Deductive reasoning is the process of arriving at a conclusion based on other statements that are all known to be true.

A symbolic argument consists of a set of premises and a conclusion in the format of of *if* [premise 1 and premise 2], *then* [conclusion].

An argument is **valid** when the conclusion follows necessarily from the premises. An argument is **invalid** or a fallacy when the conclusion does not follow from the premises.

Four standard forms of valid arguments must be remembered.

1. Law of Detachment   If p, then q (premise 1)
                                p (premise 2)
                                Therefore, q

2. Law of Contraposition   If p, then q
                                not q
                                Therefore, not p

3. Law of Syllogism   If p, then q
                                If q, then r
                                Therefore if p, then r

4. Disjunctive Syllogism p or q
                                  not p
                                Therefore, q

Example: Can a conclusion be reached from these two statements?

    A.   All swimmers are athletes.
          All athletes are scholars.

In *if-then* form, these would be:

    If you are a swimmer, then you are an athlete.
    If you are an athlete, then you are a scholar.

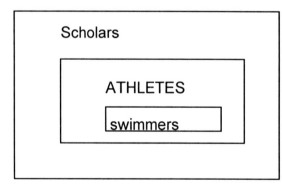

Clearly, if you are a swimmer, then you are also an athlete. This includes you in the group of scholars.

    B.   All swimmers are athletes.
          All wrestlers are athletes.

In *if-then* form, these would be:

    If you are a swimmer, then you are an athlete.
    If you are a wrestler, then you are an athlete.

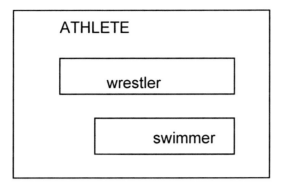

Clearly, if you are a swimmer or a wrestler, then you are also an athlete. This does NOT allow you to come to any other conclusions.

A swimmer may or may NOT also be a wrestler. Therefore, NO CONCLUSION IS POSSIBLE.

Suppose that these statements were given to you, and you were asked to try to reach a conclusion. The statements are:

Example: Determine whether statement A, B, C, or D can be deduced from the following:

(i) If John drives the big truck, then the shipment will be delivered.

(ii) The shipment will not be delivered.

a. John does not drive the big truck.
b. John drives the big truck.
c. The shipment will not be delivered.
d. None of the above conclusion is true.

Let p: John drives the big truck.
q: The shipment is delivered.

statement (i) gives $p \rightarrow q$, statement (ii) gives $\sim q$. This is the Law of Contraposition.

Therefore, the logical conclusion is $\sim p$ or "John does not drive the big truck." Therefore, the answer is response A.

Example: Given that:

(i) Peter is a jet pilot or Peter is a navigator.
(ii) Peter is not a jet pilot.

Determine which conclusion can be logically deduced.

a. Peter is not a navigator.
b. Peter is a navigator.
c. Peter is neither a jet pilot nor a navigator.
d. None of the above is true.

Let p: Peter is a jet pilot.
   q: Peter is a navigator.

So we have $p \lor q$ from statement (i)
            $\sim p$ from statement (ii)

So choose response B.

Try These:

What conclusion, if any, can be reached? Assume each statement is true, regardless of any personal beliefs.

1. If the Red Sox win the World Series, I will die.
   I died.

2. If an angle's measure is between 0° and 90°, then the angle is acute. Angle B is not acute.

3. Students who do well in geometry will succeed in college.
   Annie is doing extremely well in geometry.

4. Left-handed people are witty and charming.
   You are left-handed.

Question #1	The Red Sox won the World Series.
Question #2	Angle B is not between 0 and 90 degrees.
Question #3	Annie will do well in college.
Question #4	You are witty and charming.

Skill 10.3 **Solve word problems involving integers, fractions, decimals, and percents**

See Competency 7.0.

Skill 10.4   Apply number properties and geometric principles to solve a variety of problems

See Competency 8.0.

Skill 10.5   Evaluate an algebraic expression by substituting numbers for variables

Procedure for solving algebraic equations

Example: $3(x+3) = {}^- 2x + 4$ Solve for x.

1)   Expand to eliminate all parentheses.

$3x + 9 = {}^- 2x + 4$

2)   Multiply each term by the LCD to eliminate all denominators.

3)   Combine like terms on each side when possible.

4)   Use the properties to put all variables on one side and all constants on the other side.

$\rightarrow 3x + 9 - 9 = {}^- 2x + 4 - 9$ (subtract nine from both sides)

$\rightarrow 3x = {}^- 2x - 5$

$\rightarrow 3x + 2x = {}^- 2x + 2x - 5$ (add 2x to both sides)

$\rightarrow 5x = {}^- 5$

$\rightarrow \dfrac{5x}{5} = \dfrac{{}^- 5}{5}$ (divide both sides by 5)

$\rightarrow x = {}^- 1$

Example: Solve: $3(2x + 5) - 4x = 5(x + 9)$

$6x + 15 - 4x = 5x + 45$

$2x + 15 = 5x + 45$

${}^- 3x + 15 = 45$

${}^- 3x = 30$

$x = {}^- 10$

The solution **set of linear equations** is all the ordered pairs of real numbers that satisfy both equations, thus the intersection of the lines. There are two methods for solving linear equations: **linear combinations** and **substitution**.

In the **substitution** method, an equation is solved for either variable. Then, that solution is substituted in the other equation to find the remaining variable.

Example:

(1) $2x + 8y = 4$
(2) $x - 3y = 5$

(2a) $x = 3y + 5$ Solve equation (2) for x

(1a) $2(3y + 5) + 8y = 4$ Substitute x in equation (1)
         $6y + 10 + 8y = 4$ Solve.
         $14y = -6$
         $y = \frac{-3}{7}$ Solution

(2) $x - 3y = 5$
      $x - 3(\frac{-3}{7}) = 5$ Substitute the value of y.
      $x = \frac{26}{7} = 3\frac{5}{7}$ Solution

Thus, the solution set of the system of equations is $(3\frac{5}{7}, \frac{-3}{7})$.

In the **linear combinations** method, one or both of the equations are replaced with an equivalent equation in order that the two equations can be combined (added or subtracted) to eliminate one variable.

Example:

(1) $4x + 3y = -2$
(2) $5x - y = 7$

(1) $4x + 3y = -2$
(2a) $15x - 3y = 21$ Multiply equation (2) by 3

$19x = 19$ Combining (1) and (2a)
$x = 1$ Solve.

To find y, substitute the value of x in equation 1 (or 2).

(1) $4x + 3y = -2$
      $4(1) + 3y = -2$
      $4 + 3y = -2$
      $3y = -2$
      $y = -2$

Thus, the solution is $x = 1$ and $y = -2$ or the ordered pair $(1, -2)$.

Example: Solve for x and y.

$$4x + 6y = 340$$
$$3x + 8y = 360$$

To solve by addition-subtraction:

Multiply the first equation by 4: $4(4x + 6y = 340)$

Multiply the other equation by $^-3$: $^-3(3x + 8y = 360)$

By doing this, the equations can be added to each other to eliminate one variable and solve for the other variable.

$$16x + 24y = 1360$$
$$\underline{-9x - 24y = {}^-1080}$$
$$7x = 280$$
$$x = 40$$

solving for y, $y = 30$

Skill 10.6   Solve algebraic equations and inequalities

Procedure for solving algebraic inequalities

We use the same procedure used for solving linear equations, but the answer is represented in graphical form on the number line or in interval form.

Example: Solve the inequality, show its solution using interval form, and graph the solution on the number line.

$$\frac{5x}{8} + 3 \geq 2x - 5$$

$$8\left(\frac{5x}{8}\right) + 8(3) \geq 8(2x) - 5(8) \qquad \text{Multiply by LCD = 8.}$$

$$5x + 24 \geq 16x - 40$$

$$5x + 24 - 24 - 16x \geq 16x - 16x - 40 - 24$$

Subtract 16x and 24 from both sides of the equation.

$$^-11x \geq ^- 64$$

$$\frac{^-11x}{^-11} \leq \frac{^-64}{^-11}$$

$$x \leq \frac{64}{11} \quad ; \quad x \leq 5\frac{9}{11}$$

Solution in interval form: $\left(^-\infty, 5\frac{9}{11}\right]$

Note: "] " means $5\frac{9}{11}$ is included in the solution.

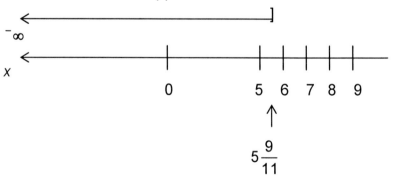

Example: Solve the following inequality and express your answer in both interval and graphical form.

$$3x - 8 < 2(3x - 1)$$

$$3x - 8 < 6x - 2$$ Distributive property.

$$3x - 6x - 8 + 8 < 6x - 6x - 2 + 8$$

Add 8 and subtract 6x from both sides of the equation.

$$^-3x < 6$$

$$\frac{^-3x}{^-3} > \frac{6}{^-3}$$ Note the change in direction of the equality.

$$x > ^- 2$$

Graphical form:

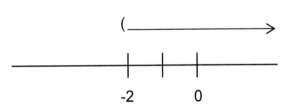

or

Interval form: $(^-2, \infty)$

Recall that using a parentheses or an open circle implies the point is not included in the answer and using a bracket or a closed circle implies the point is included in the answer.

Example: Solve: $6x + 21 < 8x + 31$

$$^-2x + 21 < 31$$

$$^-2x < 10$$

$$x > ^-5$$

          Note that the inequality sign has changed.

Absolute value equations and equalities

If *a* and *b* are real numbers, and *k* is a non-negative real number, the solution of

$$|ax + b| = k \quad \text{is} \quad ax + b = k \quad \text{or} \quad ax + b = ^- k$$

$$|ax + b| > k \quad \text{is} \quad ax + b > k \quad \text{or} \quad ax + b < ^- k$$

Example: $|2x + 3| = 9$ solve for *x*.

$2x + 3 = 9$	or	$2x + 3 = ^- 9$
$2x + 3 - 3 = 9 - 3$	or	$2x + 3 - 3 = ^- 9 - 3$
$2x = 6$	or	$2x = ^- 12$
$\dfrac{2x}{2} = \dfrac{6}{2}$	or	$\dfrac{2x}{2} = \dfrac{^-12}{2}$
$x = 3$	or	$x = ^- 6$

Therefore, the solution is $x = \{3, ^- 6\}$

Example: Solve $|7x + 3| < 25$

$$^-25 < (7x + 3) < 25$$

$$(^-25 - 3) < (7x) < (25 - 3)$$

Subtract 3 from all sides.

$$^-28 < 7x < 22$$

$$^-4 < x < \frac{22}{7}$$

Divide all terms by 7.

Solution in interval form is $\left(^-4, \dfrac{22}{7} \right)$

Solution in graphical form:

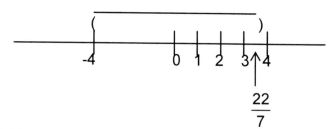

See also Skill 10.5.

Skill 10.7   Estimate results and determine reasonableness

To estimate measurement of familiar objects, it is first necessary to determine the units to be used.

<u>Examples:</u>

Length
1. The coastline of Florida
2. The width of a ribbon
3. The thickness of a book
4. The depth of water in a pool

Weight or mass
1. A bag of sugar
2. A school bus
3. A dime

Capacity or volume
1. Paint to paint a bedroom
2. Glass of milk

Money
1. Cost of a house
2. Cost of a cup of coffee
3. Exchange rate

Perimeter
1. The edge of a backyard
2. The edge of a football field

Area
1. The size of a carpet
2. The size of a state

Example: Estimate the measurements of the following objects:

Length of a dollar bill	6 inches
Weight of a baseball	1 pound
Distance from New York to Florida	1100 km
Volume of water to fill a medicine dropper	1 milliliter
Length of a desk	2 meters
Temperature of water in a swimming pool	80° F

Depending on the degree of accuracy needed, an object may be measured to different units. For example, a pencil may be 6 inches to the nearest inch, or 6 3/8 inches to the nearest eighth of an inch. Similarly, it might be 15 cm to the nearest centimeter or 154 mm to the nearest millimeter.

Given a set of objects and their measurements, the use of rounding procedures is helpful when attempting to round to the nearest given unit. When rounding to a given place value, it is necessary to look at the number in the next smaller place. If this number is 5 or more, the number in the place we are rounding to is increased by one and all numbers to the right are changed to zero. If the number is less than 5, the number in the place we are rounding to stays the same and all numbers to the right are changed to zero.

One method of rounding measurements can require an additional step. First, the measurement must be converted to a decimal number. Then the rules for rounding apply.

Example: Round the measurements to the given units.

MEASUREMENT	ROUND TO NEAREST	ANSWER
1 foot 7 inches	foot	2 ft
5 pound 6 ounces	pound	5 pounds
5 9/16 inches	inch	6 inches

Convert each measurement to a decimal number. Then apply the rules for rounding.

1 foot 7 inches = $1\frac{7}{12}$ ft = 1.58333 ft, round up to 2 ft

5 pounds 6 ounces = $5\frac{6}{16}$ pounds = 5.375 pound, round to 5 pounds

$5\frac{9}{16}$ inches = 5.5625 inches, round up to 6 inches

Example: Janet goes into a store to purchase a CD on sale for $13.95. While shopping, she sees two pairs of shoes, prices $19.95 and $14.50. She only has $50. Can she purchase everything?

Solve by rounding:

$19.95→$20.00
$14.50→$15.00
$13.95→$14.00
$49.00   Yes, she can purchase the CD and the shoes.

Sample Test: Mathematics

1. $0.74 =$
(Easy) (Skill 7.1)

A. $\dfrac{74}{100}$

B. 7.4%

C. $\dfrac{33}{50}$

D. $\dfrac{74}{10}$

2. What is the greatest common factor of 16, 28, and 36?
(Easy) (Skill 7.1)

A. 2

B. 4

C. 8

D. 16

3. $\dfrac{2^{10}}{2^5} =$
(Rigorous) (Skill 7.1)

A. 2^2

B. 2^5

C. 2^{50}

D. $2^{\frac{1}{2}}$

4. Which of the following sets of numbers is all integers?
(Easy) (Skill 7.1)

A. 0, 1, 6, 7, 8, 13, 14

B. $2\dfrac{1}{4}, \ ^-5\dfrac{1}{6}, \ 7\dfrac{1}{3}$

C. $\sqrt{5} = 2.2360\ldots$

D. $-25, -17, -12, 3, 6, 12$

5. $\left(\dfrac{^-4}{9}\right) + \left(\dfrac{^-7}{10}\right) =$
(Average Rigor) (Skill 7.2)

A. $\dfrac{23}{90}$

B. $\dfrac{^-23}{90}$

C. $\dfrac{103}{90}$

D. $\dfrac{^-103}{90}$

6. $(5.6) \times (^-0.11) =$
(Average Rigor) (Skill 7.2)

A. $^-0.616$

B. 0.616

C. $^-6.110$

D. 6.110

7. $(3 \times 9)^4 =$
   (Rigorous) (Skill 7.2)

   A. $(3 \times 9)(3 \times 9)(27 \times 27)$

   B. $(3 \times 9) + (3 \times 9)$

   C. (12×36)

   D. $(3 \times 9) + (3 \times 9) + (3 \times 9) + (3 \times 9)$

8. $4\frac{2}{9} \times \frac{7}{10}$
   (Rigorous) (Skill 7.2)

   A. $4\frac{9}{10}$

   B. $\frac{266}{90}$

   C. $2\frac{43}{45}$

   D. $2\frac{6}{20}$

9. $^-9\frac{1}{4}$ ☐ $^-8\frac{2}{3}$
   (Average Rigor) (Skill 7.2)

   A. $=$

   B. $<$

   C. $>$

   D. $\leq$

10. 303 is what percent of 600?
    (Easy) (Skill 7.2)

    A. 0.505%

    B. 5.05%

    C. 505%

    D. 50.5%

11. An item that sells for $375 is put on sale at $120. What is the percent of decrease? (Average Rigor) (Skill 7.2)

    A. 25%

    B. 28%

    C. 68%

    D. 34%

12. A sofa sells for $520. If the retailer makes a 30% profit, what was the wholesale price?
    (Average Rigor) (Skill 7.2)

    A. $400

    B. $676

    C. $490

    D. $364

13. Choose the expression that is not equivalent to 5x + 3y + 15z:
(Average Rigor) (Skill 7.3)

   A.   5(x + 3z) + 3y

   B.   3(x + y + 5z)

   C.   3y + 5(x + 3z)

   D.   5x + 3(y + 5z)

14. $\dfrac{7}{9} + \dfrac{1}{3} \div \dfrac{2}{3} =$
(Average Rigor) (Skill 7.3)

   A. $\dfrac{5}{3}$

   B. $\dfrac{3}{2}$

   C.   2

   D. $\dfrac{23}{18}$

15. $(^{-}2.1 \times 10^4)(4.2 \times 10^{-5}) =$
(Rigorous) (Skill 7.3)

   A.   8.82

   B.   -8.82

   C.   -0.882

   D.   0.882

16. If $4x - (3 - x) = 7(x - 3) + 10$, then
(Average Rigor) (Skill 7.3)

   A. $x = 8$

   B. $x = -8$

   C. $x = 4$

   D. $x = -4$

17. What measure could be used to report the distance traveled in walking around a track?
(Easy) (Skill 8.1)

   A.   degrees

   B.   square meters

   C.   kilometers

   D.   cubic feet

18. What unit of measurement would describe the spread of a forest fire in a unit time?
(Average Rigor) (Skill 8.1)

   A.   10 square yards per second

   B.   10 yards per minute

   C.   10 feet per hour

   D.   10 cubit feet per hour

19. A boy walked three miles during a charity event. How far did he walk?
(Easy) (Skill 8.2)

   A.   4827 km

   B.   48.27 m

   C.   4.83 km

   D.   5280 feet

20. For the following statements

   I.   All parallelograms are rectangles
   II.   Some rhombuses are squares
   III. All parallelograms are rectangles
   (Average Rigor) (Skill 8.3)

   A.   All statements are correct

   B.   All statements are incorrect

   C.   Only II and III are correct

   D.   Only II is correct

21. What type of triangle is △***ABC*** ?
(Average Rigor) (Skill 8.4)

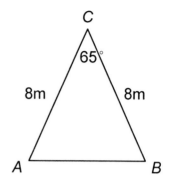

   A.   right

   B.   equilateral

   C.   scalene

   D.   isosceles

22. Study figures A, B, C, and D. Select the letter in which all triangles are similar. (Rigorous) (Skill 8.4)

A.

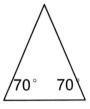

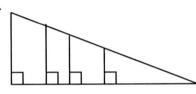

B.

C.

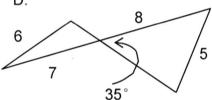

D.

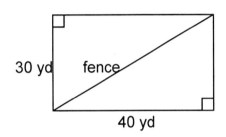

23. A cone is a figure that has which of the following characteristics? (Easy) (Skill 8.4)

  A.   two congruent circular bases that are parallel

  B.   a circular base and a single vertex

  C.   all points are the same distance from the center

  D.   a square base and 4 triangle-shaped sides

24. The owner of a rectangular piece of land 40 yards in length and 30 yards in width wants to divide it into two parts. She plans to join two opposite corners with a fence as shown in the diagram below. The cost of the fence will be approximately $25 per linear foot. What is the estimated cost for the fence needed by the owner? (Rigorous) (Skill 8.5)

  A. $1,250

  B. $62,500

  C. $5,250

  D. $3,750

25. What is the area of a square whose side is 13 feet? (Average Rigor) (Skill 8.5)

  A.   169 feet

  B.   169 square feet

  C.   52 feet

  D.   52 square feet

26. The trunk of a tree has a 2.1-meter radius. What is its circumference?
(Rigorous) (Skill 8.5)

   A. 2.1π square meters

   B. 4.2π meters

   C. 2.1π meters

   D. 4.2π square meters

27. What is the area of this triangle?
(Rigorous) (Skill 8.5)

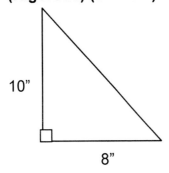

   A.   80 square inches

   B.   20 square inches

   C.   40 square inches

   D.   30 square inches

28. The following chart shows the yearly average number of international tourists visiting Palm Beach for 1990-1994. How many more international tourists visited Palm Beach in 1994 than in 1991?
(Easy) (Skill 9.1)

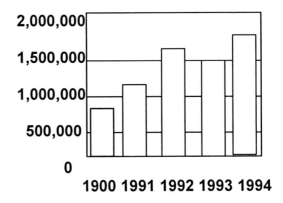

   A.   100,000

   B.   600,000

   C.   1,600,000

   D.   8,000,000

29. Consider the graph of the distribution of the length of time it took individuals to complete an employment form.
(Easy) (Skill 9.1)

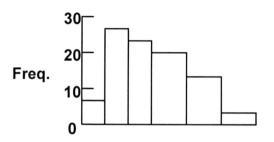

Approximately how many individuals took less than 15 minutes to complete the employment form?

A.   35
B.   28
C.   7
D.   4

30. Which statement is true about George's budget?
(Easy) (Skill 9.1)

A. George spends the greatest portion of his income on food.

B. George spends twice as much on utilities as he does on his mortgage.

C. George spends twice as much on utilities as he does on food.

D. George spends the same amount on food and utilities as he does on mortgage.

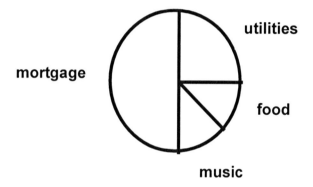

31. The table below shows the distribution of majors for a group of college students.

Major	Proportion of students
Mathematics	0.32
Photography	0.26
Journalism	0.19
Engineering	0.21
Criminal Law	0.02

If it is known that a student chosen at random is not majoring in mathematics or engineering, what is the probability that a student is majoring in journalism? (Rigorous) (Skill 9.2)

A. 0.19

B. 0.36

C. 0.40

D. 0.81

32. What is the probability of drawing 2 consecutive aces from a standard deck of cards? (Rigorous) (Skill 9.2)

A. $\frac{3}{51}$

B. $\frac{1}{221}$

C. $\frac{2}{104}$

D. $\frac{2}{52}$

33. Given a drawer with 5 black socks, 3 blue socks, and 2 red socks, what is the probability that you will draw two black socks in two draws in a dark room? (Rigorous) (Skill 9.2)

A. 2/9

B. 1/4

C. 17/18

D. 1/18

34. What is the mode of the data in the following sample? (Average Rigor) (Skill 9.3)

9, 10, 11, 9, 10, 11, 9, 13

A. 9

B. 9.5

C. 10

D. 11

35. Mary did comparison shopping on her favorite brand of coffee. Over half of the stores priced the coffee at $1.70. Most of the remaining stores priced the coffee at $1.80, except for a few who charged $1.90. Which of the following statements is true about the distribution of prices? (Rigorous) (Skill 9.3)

A. The mean and the mode are the same.
B. The mean is greater than the mode.
C. The mean is less than the mode.
D. The mean is less than the median.

36. Corporate salaries are listed for several employees. Which would be the best measure of central tendency? (Rigorous) (Skill 9.3)

$24,000 $24,000 $26,000
$28,000 $30,000 $120,000

A. mean
B. median
C. mode
D. no difference

37. A student organization is interested in determining how strong the support is among registered voters in the United States for the president's education plan. Which of the following procedures would be most appropriate for selecting a statistically unbiased sample? (Rigorous) (Skill 9.4)

A. Having viewers call in to a nationally broadcast talk show and give their opinions.

B. Survey registered voters selected by blind drawing in the three largest states.

C. Select regions of the country by blind drawing and then select people from the voters registration list by blind drawing.

D. Pass out survey forms at the front entrance of schools selected by blind drawing and ask people entering and exiting to fill them in.

38. Two mathematics classes have a total of 410 students. The 8:00 am class has 40 more than the 10:00 am class. How many students are in the 10:00 am class? (Rigorous) (Skill 10.1)

A. 123.3

B. 370

C. 185

D. 330

39. Identify the missing term in the following harmonic sequence:
(Easy) (Skill 10.1)

$$\frac{1}{3}, \frac{1}{6}, \frac{1}{9}, \frac{1}{12}, \frac{1}{15}, ?$$

A. $\frac{1}{16}$

B. $\frac{1}{17}$

C. $\frac{1}{18}$

D. 18

40. Set A, B, C, and U are related as shown in the diagram.

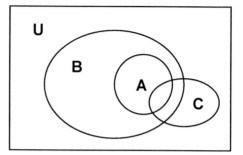

Which of the following is true, assuming not one of the six regions is empty? (Average Rigor) (Skill 10.2)

A. Any element that is a member of set B is also a member of set A.

B. No element is a member of all three sets A, B, and C.

C. Any element that is a member of set U is also a member of set B.

D. None of the above statements is true.

41. **Select the statement that is the negation of the statement, "If the weather is cold, then the soccer game will be played."**
(Average Rigor) (Skill 10.2)

A.   If the weather is not cold, then the soccer game will be played.

B.   The weather is cold and the soccer game was not played.

C.   If the soccer game is played, then the weather is not cold.

D.   The weather is cold and the soccer game will be played.

42. **Select the statement below that is NOT logically equivalent to "If Mary works late, then Bill will prepare lunch."**
(Average Rigor) (Skill 10.2)

A.   Bill prepares lunch or Mary does not work late.

B.   If Bill does not prepare lunch, then Mary did not work late.

C.   If Bill prepares lunch, then Mary works late.

D.   Mary does not work late or Bill prepares lunch.

43. **Select the rule of logical equivalence that directly (in one step) transforms the statement (i) into statement (ii).**

i.   Not all the students have books.
ii. Some students do not have books.
(Average Rigor) (Skill 10.2)

A.   "If p, then q" is equivalent to "if not q, then p."

B.   "Not all are p" is equivalent to "some are not p."

C.   "Not q" is equivalent to "p."

D.   "All are not p" is equivalent to "none is p."

44. Given that:
    i. No athletes are weak.
    ii. All football players are athletes.

    Determine which conclusion can be logically deduced.
    (Average Rigor) (Skill 10.2)

    A. Some football players are weak.

    B. All football players are weak.

    C. No football player is weak.

    D. None of the above is true.

45. All of the following arguments have true conclusions, but one of the arguments is not valid. Select the argument that is not valid.
    (Average Rigor) (Skill 10.2)

    A. All sea stars are echinoderms and all echinoderms are marine; therefore, all sea stars are marine.

    B. All spiders are dangerous. The black widow is dangerous. Therefore, the black widow is a spider.

    C. All crocodiles are amphibians and all amphibians breathe by lungs, gill, or skin; therefore, all crocodiles breathe by lungs, gill, or skin.

    D. All kids have hats and all boys are kids; therefore, all boys have hats.

46. Study the information given below. If a logical conclusion is given, select that conclusion.

Bob eats donuts or he eats yogurt. If Bob eats yogurt, then he is healthy. If Bob is healthy, then he can run the marathon. Bob does not eat yogurt.
(Average Rigor) (Skill 10.2)

A. Bob does not eat donuts.

B. Bob is healthy.

C. If Bob runs the Marathon, then he eats yogurt.

D. None of the above is warranted.

47. A restaurant employs 465 people. There are 280 waiters and 185 cooks. If 168 waiters and 85 cooks receive pay raises, what percent of the waiters will receive a pay raise?
(Average Rigor) (Skill 10.3)

A. 36.13%

B. 60%

C. 60.22%

D. 40%

48. Given the formula $d = rt$, (where d = distance, r = rate, and t = time), calculate the time required for a vehicle to travel 585 miles at a rate of 65 miles per hour.
(Average Rigor) (Skill 10.3)

A. 8.5 hours

B. 6.5 hours

C. 9.5 hours

D. 9 hours

49. The price of gas was $3.27 per gallon. Your tank holds 15 gallons of fuel. You are using two tanks a week. How much will you save weekly if the price of gas goes down to $2.30 per gallon?
(Average Rigor) (Skill 10.3)

A. $26.00

B. $29.00

C. $15.00

D. $17.00

50. It takes 5 equally skilled people 9 hours to shingle Mr. Joe's roof. Let t be the time required for only 3 of these men to do the same job. Select the correct statement of the given condition.
(Rigorous) (Skill 10.3)

A. $\dfrac{3}{5} = \dfrac{9}{t}$

B. $\dfrac{9}{5} = \dfrac{3}{t}$

C. $\dfrac{5}{9} = \dfrac{3}{t}$

D. $\dfrac{14}{9} = \dfrac{t}{5}$

51. In a sample of 40 full-time employees at a particular company, 35 were also holding down a part-time job requiring at least 10 hours/week. If this proportion holds for the entire company of 25,000 employees, how many full-time employees at this company are actually holding down a part-time job of at least 10 hours per week.
(Rigorous) (Skill 10.3)

A. 714

B. 625

C. 21,875

D. 28,571

52. For each of the statements below, determine whether $x = \dfrac{1}{6}$ is a solution.

i. $6x \le 4x^2 + 2$
ii. $10x + 1 = 3(4x - 3)$
iii. $|x - 1| = x$
(Rigorous) (Skill 10.5)

A. i, ii, and iii

B. i and iii only

C. i only

D. iii only

53. Given $f(x) = (x)^3 - 3(x)^2 + 5$, find $x = (-2)$.
(Rigorous) (Skill 10.5)

A. 15

B. -15

C. 25

D. -25

54. Choose the equation that is equivalent to the following:
(Rigorous) (Skill 10.5)

$$\dfrac{3x}{5} - 5 = 5x$$

A. $3x - 25 = 25x$

B. $x - \dfrac{25}{3} = 25x$

C. $6x - 50 = 75x$

D. $x + 25 = 25x$

55. What is the equation that expresses the relationship between x and y in the table below?
(Rigorous) (Skill 10.5)

x	y
-2	4
-1	2
0	-2
1	-5
2	-8

A. y = -x - 2

B. y = -3x - 2

C. y = 3x - 2

D. $y = \frac{1}{3}x - 1$

56. The figure below shows a running track in the shape of a rectangle with semicircles at each end.
(Rigorous) (Skill 10.6)

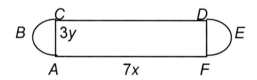

Calculate the distance around the track.

A. $6\pi y + 14x$

B. $3\pi y + 7x$

C. $6\pi y + 7x$

D. $3\pi y + 14x$

57. Choose the statement that is true for all real numbers.
(Rigorous) (Skill 10.6)

A. $a = 0, b \neq 0,$ then $\frac{b}{a} =$ undefined.

B. $^-(a + (^-a)) = 2a$

C. $2(ab) = ^- (2a)b$

D. $^-a(b + 1) = ab - a$

58. Solve for x.
$$3x - \frac{2}{3} = \frac{5x}{2} + 2$$
(Rigorous) (Skill 10.6)

A. $5\frac{1}{3}$

B. $\frac{17}{3}$

C. 2

D. $\frac{16}{2}$

59. A car gets 25.36 miles per gallon. The car has been driven 83,310 miles. What is a reasonable estimate for the number of gallons of gas used?
(Average Rigor) (Skill 10.7)

   A. 2,087 gallons

   B. 3,000 gallons

   C. 1,800 gallons

   D. 164 gallons

60. Round $1\frac{13}{16}$ of an inch to the nearest quarter of an inch.
(Easy) (Skill 10.7)

   A. $1\frac{1}{4}$ inch

   B. $1\frac{5}{8}$ inch

   C. $1\frac{3}{4}$ inch

   D. 2 inches

Answer Key: Mathematics

1.	A		31.	C
2.	B		32.	B
3.	B		33.	A
4.	D		34.	A
5.	D		35.	B
6.	A		36.	B
7.	A		37.	C
8.	C		38.	C
9.	B		39.	C
10.	A		40.	D
11.	C		41.	A
12.	A		42.	C
13.	B		43.	B
14.	D		44.	C
15.	C		45.	B
16.	C		46.	D
17.	C		47.	B
18.	A		48.	D
19.	C		49.	B
20.	D		50.	B
21.	D		51.	C
22.	B		52.	C
23.	B		53.	B
24.	D		54.	A
25.	B		55.	B
26.	B		56.	D
27.	C		57.	A
28.	B		58.	A
29.	C		59.	B
30.	C		60.	C

Rigor Table

	Easy 20%	Average 40%	Rigorous 40%
Questions (60)	1, 2, 4, 10, 17, 19, 23, 28, 29, 30, 39, 60	5, 6, 9, 11, 12, 13, 14, 16, 18, 20, 21, 25, 34, 40, 41, 42, 43, 44, 45, 46, 47, 48, 49, 59	3, 7, 8, 15, 22, 24, 26, 27, 31, 32, 33, 35, 36, 37, 38, 50, 51, 52, 53, 54, 55, 56, 57, 58
TOTALS	12 (20%)	24 (40%)	24 (40%)

Rationales with Sample Questions: Mathematics

1. **0.74 =**
    (Easy) (Skill 7.1)

    A. $\dfrac{74}{100}$

    B. 7.4%

    C. $\dfrac{33}{50}$

    D. $\dfrac{74}{10}$

Answer: A. $\dfrac{74}{100}$

This is basic conversion of decimals to fractions. 0.74→the 4 is in the hundredths place, so the answer is $\dfrac{74}{100}$.

2. **What is the greatest common factor of 16, 28, and 36?**
    (Easy) (Skill 7.1)

    A. 2

    B. 4

    C. 8

    D. 16

Answer: B. 4

The smallest number in this set is 16; its factors are 1, 2, 4, 8, and 16. Sixteen is the largest factor, but it does not divide into 28 or 36. Neither does 8. Four does factor into both 28 and 36.

3. $\dfrac{2^{10}}{2^5} =$

    (Rigorous) (Skill 7.1)

    A. 2^2

    B. 2^5

    C. 2^{50}

    D. $2^{\frac{1}{2}}$

Answer: B. 2^5

The quotient rule of exponents says $\dfrac{a^m}{a^n} = a^{(m-n)}$ so $\dfrac{2^{10}}{2^5} = 2^{(10-5)} = 2^5$.

4. **Which of the following sets of numbers is all integers?**
    (Easy) (Skill 7.1)

    A. 0, 1, 6, 7, 8, 13, 14

    B. $2\dfrac{1}{4}, \ ^-5\dfrac{1}{6}, \ 7\dfrac{1}{3}$

    C. $\sqrt{5} = 2.2360...$

    D. −25, −17, −12, 3, 6, 12

Answer: D. −25, −17, −12, 3, 6, 12

Answer A lists whole numbers, B lists mixed numbers, and C lists irrational numbers. D lists integers.

5. $\left(\dfrac{^-4}{9}\right) + \left(\dfrac{^-7}{10}\right) =$

(Average Rigor) (Skill 7.2)

A. $\dfrac{23}{90}$

B. $\dfrac{^-23}{90}$

C. $\dfrac{103}{90}$

D. $\dfrac{^-103}{90}$

Answer: D. $\dfrac{^-103}{90}$

Find the LCD of $\dfrac{^-4}{9}$ and $\dfrac{^-7}{10}$. The LCD is 90, so you get $\dfrac{^-40}{90} + \dfrac{^-63}{90} = \dfrac{^-103}{90}$.

6. $(5.6) \times \left(^-0.11\right) =$

(Average Rigor) (Skill 7.2)

A. $^-0.616$

B. 0.616

C. $^-6.110$

D. 6.110

Answer: A. –0.616

Simple multiplication. The answer will be negative because a positive times a negative is a negative number. $5.6 \times ^- 0.11 =^- 0.616$.

7. $(3 \times 9)^4 =$
        (Rigorous) (Skill 7.2)

        A. $(3 \times 9)(3 \times 9)(27 \times 27)$

        B. $(3 \times 9) + (3 \times 9)$

        C. (12×36)

        D. $(3 \times 9) + (3 \times 9) + (3 \times 9)$
                $+ (3 \times 9)$

Answer: A. (3 x 9) (3 x 9) (27 x 27)

$(3 \times 9)^4 = (3 \times 9)(3 \times 9)(3 \times 9)(3 \times 9)$, which, when solving two of the parentheses, is $(3 \times 9)(3 \times 9)(27 \times 27)$.

8. $4\dfrac{2}{9} \; x \; \dfrac{7}{10}$
        (Rigorous) (Skill 7.2)

        A. $4\dfrac{9}{10}$

        B. $\dfrac{266}{90}$

        C. $2\dfrac{43}{45}$

        D. $2\dfrac{6}{20}$

Answer: C. $2\dfrac{43}{45}$

Convert any mixed number to an improper fraction: $\dfrac{38}{9} \, x \, \dfrac{7}{10}$. Since no common factors of numerators or denominators exist, multiply the numerators and the denominators by each other = $\dfrac{266}{90}$. Convert back to a mixed number and reduce $2\dfrac{86}{90} = 2\dfrac{43}{45}$.

9. $-9\dfrac{1}{4}$ ☐ $-8\dfrac{2}{3}$
    (Average Rigor) (Skill 7.2)

    A. =

    B. <

    C. >

    D. ≤

Answer: B. <

The larger the absolute value of a negative number, the smaller the negative number is. The absolute value of $-9\dfrac{1}{4}$ is $9\dfrac{1}{4}$ which is larger than the absolute value of $-8\dfrac{2}{3}$ is $8\dfrac{2}{3}$. Therefore, the sign should be $-9\dfrac{1}{4} < -8\dfrac{2}{3}$.

10. **303 is what percent of 600?**
    (Easy) (Skill 7.2)

    A. 0.505%

    B. 5.05%

    C. 505%

    D. 50.5%

Answer: D. 50.5%

Use x for the percent. $600x = 303$. $\dfrac{600x}{600} = \dfrac{303}{600} \rightarrow x = 0.505 = 50.5\%$.

11. An item that sells for $375 is put on sale at $120. What is the percent of decrease?
(Average Rigor) (Skill 7.2)

   A. 25%

   B. 28%

   C. 68%

   D. 34%

Answer: C. 68%

Use $(1 - x)$ as the discount. $375x = 120$.
$375(1-x) = 120 \rightarrow 375 - 375x = 120 \rightarrow 375x = 255 \rightarrow x = 0.68 = 68\%$.

12. A sofa sells for $520. If the retailer makes a 30% profit, what was the wholesale price?
(Average Rigor) (Skill 7.2)

   A. $400

   B. $676

   C. $490

   D. $364

Answer: A. $400

Let x be the wholesale price, then x + .30x = 520, 1.30x = 520. Divide both sides by 1.30.

13. **Choose the expression that is not equivalent to 5x + 3y + 15z.**
    (Average Rigor) (Skill 7.3)

    A.   5(x + 3z) + 3y

    B.   3(x + y + 5z)

    C.   3y + 5(x + 3z)

    D.   5x + 3(y + 5z)

Answer: B. 3(x + y + 5z)

$$5x + 3y + 15z = (5x + 15z) + 3y = 5(x + 3z) + 3y \qquad \text{A. is true}$$
$$= 5x + (3y + 15z) = 5x + 3(y + 5z) \qquad \text{D. is true}$$
$$= 37 + (5x + 15z) = 37 + 5(x + 3z) \qquad \text{C. is true}$$

These can all be solved using the associative property and then factoring. However, in B, 3(x + y + 5z) by distributive property = 3x + 3y + 15z does not equal 5x + 37 + 15z.

14. $\dfrac{7}{9} + \dfrac{1}{3} \div \dfrac{2}{3} =$
      (Average Rigor) (Skill 7.3)

      A. $\dfrac{5}{3}$

      B. $\dfrac{3}{2}$

      C.   2

      D. $\dfrac{23}{18}$

Answer: D. $\dfrac{23}{18}$

First, do the division.
$$\frac{1}{3} \div \frac{2}{3} = \frac{1}{3} \times \frac{3}{2} = \frac{1}{2}$$

Next, add the fractions.
$$\frac{7}{9} + \frac{1}{2} = \frac{14}{18} + \frac{9}{18} = \frac{23}{18}, \text{ which is answer D.}$$

15. $(^-2.1 \times 10^4)(4.2 \times 10^{^-5}) =$
(Rigorous) (Skill 7.3)

    A.   8.82

    B.   -8.82

    C.   -0.882

    D.   0.882

Answer: C. –0.882

First, multiply –2.1 and 4.2 to get –8.82. Then, multiply 10^4 by $10^{^-5}$ to get $10^{^-1}$. $^-8.82 \times 10^{^-1} = ^- 0.882$.

16. If $4x - (3 - x) = 7(x - 3) + 10$, then
(Average Rigor) (Skill 7.3)

    A. $x = 8$

    B. $x = -8$

    C. $x = 4$

    D. $x = -4$

Answer: C. x = 4

Solve for x.

$$4x - (3 - x) = 7(x - 3) + 10$$
$$4x - 3 + x = 7x - 21 + 10$$
$$5x - 3 = 7x - 11$$
$$5x = 7x - 11 + 3$$
$$5x - 7x = ^- 8$$
$$^-2x = ^- 8$$
$$x = 4$$

17. **What measure could be used to report the distance traveled in walking around a track?**
(Easy) (Skill 8.1)

    A.   degrees

    B.   square meters

    C.   kilometers

    D.   cubic feet

Answer: C. kilometers

Degrees measure angles, square meters measure area, cubic feet measure volume, and kilometers measure length. Kilometers is the only reasonable answer.

18. **What unit of measurement would describe the spread of a forest fire in a unit time?**
(Average Rigor) (Skill 8.1)

    A.   10 square yards per second

    B.   10 yards per minute

    C.   10 feet per hour

    D.   10 cubit feet per hour

Answer: A. 10 square yards per second

The only appropriate answer is one that describes "an area" of forest consumed per unit time. Not all answers are units of area measurement, except answer A.

19. **A boy walked three miles during a charity event. How far did he walk?**
   (Easy) (Skill 8.2)

   A.   4827 km

   B.   48.27 m

   C.   4.83 km

   D.   5280 feet

Answer: C. 4.83 km

There are 1.61 kilometers in a mile. 1.61 x 3 = 4.83 km.

20. **Read the following statements:**

   I.   **All parallelograms are rectangles.**
   II.   **Some rhombuses are squares.**
   III.   **All parallelograms are rectangles.**
   (Average Rigor) (Skill 8.3)

   A.   All statements are correct.

   B.   All statements are incorrect.

   C.   Only II and III are correct.

   D.   Only II is correct.

Answer: D. Only II is correct.

I is false because only some parallelograms are rectangles. II is true. III is false because only some parallelograms are rhombuses. Only II is correct.

21. **What type of triangle is** △*ABC* **?**
     (Average Rigor) (Skill 8.4)

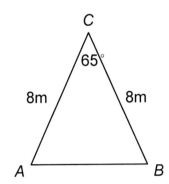

A.   right

B.   equilateral

C.   scalene

D.   isosceles

Answer: D. isosceles

Two of the sides are the same length, so we know the triangle is either equilateral or isosceles. ∡*CAB* and ∡*CBA* are equal, because their sides are.

Therefore, $180° = 65° - 2x = \dfrac{115°}{2} = 57.5°$. Because not all three angles are equal, the triangle is isosceles.

22.   **Study figures A, B, C, and D. Select the letter in which all triangles are similar.**
      (Rigorous) (Skill 8.4)

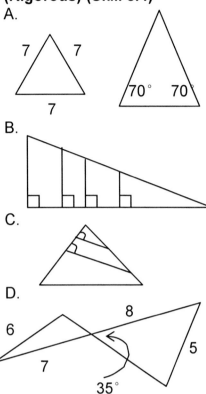

A.

B.

C.

D.

Answer: B.

Choice A is not correct because one triangle is equilateral and the other is isosceles. Choice C is not correct because the two smaller triangles are similar, but the large triangle is not. Choice D is not correct because the lengths and angles are not proportional to each other. Therefore, the correct answer is B because all the triangles have the same angles.

23.   **A cone is a figure that has which of the following characteristics?**
      (Easy) (Skill 8.4)

      A.   two congruent circular bases that are parallel

      B.   a circular base and a single vertex

      C.   all points are the same distance from the center

      D.   a square base and 4 triangle-shaped sides

Answer: B. a circular base and a single vertex
Answer A describes a cylinder; C describes a sphere; and D describes a pyramid.

24. The owner of a rectangular piece of land 40 yards in length and 30 yards in width wants to divide it into two parts. She plans to join two opposite corners with a fence as shown in the diagram below. The cost of the fence will be approximately $25 per linear foot. What is the estimated cost for the fence needed by the owner?
(Rigorous) (Skill 8.5)

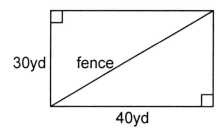

A. $1,250

B. $62,500

C. $5,250

D. $3,750

Answer: D. $3,750

Find the length of the diagonal by using the Pythagorean Theorem. Let x be the length of the diagonal.

$$30^2 + 40^2 = x^2 \rightarrow 900 + 1600 = x^2$$
$$2500 = x^2 \rightarrow \sqrt{2500} = \sqrt{x^2}$$

$$x = 50 \text{ yards}$$

Convert to feet. $\dfrac{50 \text{ yards}}{x \text{ feet}} = \dfrac{1 \text{ yard}}{3 \text{ feet}} \rightarrow 1500 \text{ feet}$

It cost $25.00 per linear foot, so the cost is (1500 ft)($25) = $3750.

25. **What is the area of a square whose side is 13 feet? (Average Rigor) (Skill 8.5)**

   A.   169 feet

   B.   169 square feet

   C.   52 feet

   D.   52 square feet

Answer: B. 169 square feet

Area = length times width (*lw*)
Length = 13 feet
Width = 13 feet (square, so length and width are the same).
Area = $13 \times 13 = 169$ square feet
Area is measured in square feet, so the answer is B.

26. **The trunk of a tree has a 2.1-meter radius. What is its circumference? (Rigorous) (Skill 8.5)**

   A. 2.1π square meters

   B. 4.2π meters

   C. $2.1 \ \pi$ meters

   D. 4.2π square meters

Answer: B. 4.2π meters

Circumference is $2\pi r$, where r is the radius. The circumference is $2\pi 2.1 = 4.2\pi$ meters (not square meters because not measuring area).

27. **What is the area of this triangle? (Rigorous) (Skill 8.5)**

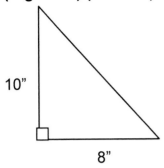

A.   80 square inches

B.   20 square inches

C.   40 square inches

D.   30 square inches

Answer: C. 40 square inches

The area of a triangle is $\frac{1}{2}bh$. $\frac{1}{2}x8x10 = 40$ square inches.

28.   The following chart shows the yearly average number of international tourists visiting Palm Beach for 1990–1994. How many more tourists that are international visited Palm Beach in 1994 than in 1991?
(Easy) (Skill 9.1)

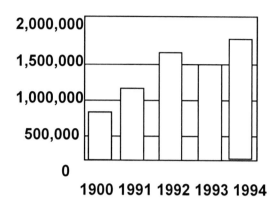

A.   100,000

B.   600,000

C.   1,600,000

D.   8,000,000

Answer: B. 600,000

The number of tourists in 1991 was 1,000,000 and the number in 1994 was 1,600,000. Subtract to get a difference of 600,000.

29. Consider the graph of the distribution of the length of time it took individuals to complete an employment form.
(Easy) (Skill 9.1)

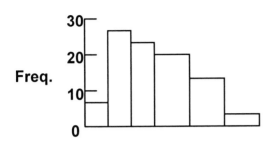

Freq.

10-14 15-19 20-24 25-29 30-34 35-39
Minutes

Approximately how many individuals took less than 15 minutes to complete the employment form?

A. 35
B. 28
C. 7
D. 4

Answer: C. 7

According to the chart, the number of people who took under 15 minutes is seven.

30.   **Which statement is true about George's budget?**
       (Easy) (Skill 9.1)

   A. George spends the greatest portion of his income on food.

   B. George spends twice as much on utilities as he does on his mortgage.

   C. George spends twice as much on utilities as he does on food.

   D. George spends the same amount on food and utilities as he does on his mortgage.

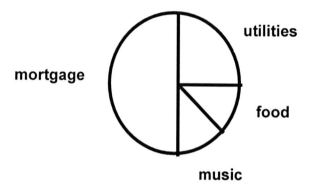

Answer: C. George spends twice as much on utilities as he does on food.

George spends the most on his mortgage, and he spends half as much on utilities as on his mortgage. Food and utilities make up one-third of his spending, while the mortgage is half. George spends twice as much on utilities as he does on food.

31. The table below shows the distribution of majors for a group of college students.

Major	Proportion of students
Mathematics	0.32
Photography	0.26
Journalism	0.19
Engineering	0.21
Criminal Law	0.02

If it is known that a student chosen at random is not majoring in mathematics or engineering, what is the probability that a student is majoring in journalism?
(Rigorous) (Skill 9.2)

A.   0.19

B.   0.36

C.   0.40

D.   0.81

Answer: C. 0.40

The proportion of students majoring in math or engineering is 0.32 + 0.21 = 0.53. This means that the proportion of students NOT majoring in math or engineering is 1.00 – 0.53 = 0.47. The proportion of students majoring in journalism out of those not majoring in math or engineering is $\frac{0.19}{0.47} = 0.404$.

32. **What is the probability of drawing two consecutive aces from a standard deck of cards?**
(Rigorous) (Skill 9.2)

    A. $\dfrac{3}{51}$

    B. $\dfrac{1}{221}$

    C. $\dfrac{2}{104}$

    D. $\dfrac{2}{52}$

Answer: B. $\dfrac{1}{221}$

There are four aces in the 52-card deck. P(first ace) = $\dfrac{4}{52}$. P(second ace) = $\dfrac{3}{51}$.

P(first ace and second ace) = P(one ace) x P(second ace|first ace) = $\dfrac{4}{52}$ x $\dfrac{3}{51}$ = $\dfrac{1}{221}$.

33. Given a drawer with 5 black socks, 3 blue socks, and 2 red socks, what is the probability that you will draw two black socks in two draws in a dark room?
(Rigorous) (Skill 9.2)

   A. 2/9

   B. 1/4

   C. 17/18

   D. 1/18

Answer: A. 2/9

In this example of conditional probability, the probability of drawing a black sock on the first draw is 5/10. It is implied in the problem that there is no replacement; therefore, the probability of obtaining a black sock in the second draw is 4/9. Multiply the two probabilities and reduce to lowest terms.

34. What is the mode of the data in the following sample?
(Average Rigor) (Skill 9.3)

   9, 10, 11, 9, 10, 11, 9, 13

   A.   9

   B.   9.5

   C.   10

   D.   11

Answer: A. 9

The mode is the number that appears most frequently. Nine appears 3 times, which is more than the other numbers.

35. Mary did comparison shopping on her favorite brand of coffee. Over half of the stores priced the coffee at $1.70. Most of the remaining stores priced the coffee at $1.80, except for a few who charged $1.90. Which of the following statements is true about the distribution of prices?
(Rigorous) (Skill 9.3)

A.   The mean and the mode are the same.
B.   The mean is greater than the mode.
C.   The mean is less than the mode.
D.   The mean is less than the median.

Answer: B. The mean is greater than the mode.

Over half the stores priced the coffee at $1.70, so this means that this is the mode. The mean would be slightly over $1.70 because other stores priced the coffee at over $1.70.

36. Corporate salaries are listed for several employees. Which would be the best measure of central tendency?
(Rigorous) (Skill 9.3)

$24,000 $24,000 $26,000 $28,000 $30,000 $120,000

A. mean
B. median
C. mode
D. no difference

Answer: B. median

The median provides the best measure of central tendency in this case where the mode is the lowest number and the mean would be disproportionately skewed by the outlier $120,000.

37. **A student organization is interested in determining how strong the support is among registered voters in the United States for the president's education plan. Which of the following procedures would be most appropriate for selecting a statistically unbiased sample? (Rigorous) (Skill 9.4)**

    A.   Having viewers call in to a nationally broadcast talk show and give their opinions.

    B.   Survey registered voters selected by blind drawing in the three largest states.

    C.   Select regions of the country by blind drawing and then select people from the voters registration list by blind drawing.

    D.   Pass out survey forms at the front entrance of schools selected by blind drawing and ask people entering and exiting to fill them in.

Answer: C. Select regions of the country by blind drawing and then select people from the voters registration list by blind drawing.

C is the best answer because it is random and it surveys a larger population.

38. **Two mathematics classes have a total of 410 students. The 8:00 am class has 40 more than the 10:00 am class. How many students are in the 10:00 am class? (Rigorous) (Skill 10.1)**

    A.   123.3

    B.   370

    C.   185

    D.   330

Answer: C. 185

Let x = # of students in the 8 am class and $x - 40$ = # of students in the 10 am class. $x + (x - 40) = 410 \rightarrow 2x - 40 = 410 \rightarrow 2x = 450 \rightarrow x = 225$. Therefore, there are 225 students in the 8 am class, and $225 - 40 = 185$ in the 10 am class.

39. **Identify the missing term in the following harmonic sequence: (Easy) (Skill 10.1)**

$$\frac{1}{3}, \frac{1}{6}, \frac{1}{9}, \frac{1}{12}, \frac{1}{15}, ?$$

A. $\frac{1}{16}$

B. $\frac{1}{17}$

C. $\frac{1}{18}$

D. 18

Answer: C. 1/18

The difference between the denominators is 3, so the next term in the progression is $\frac{1}{18}$.

40.   Set A, B, C, and U are related as shown in the diagram.

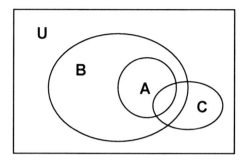

Which of the following is true, assuming not one of the six regions is empty?
(Average Rigor) (Skill 10.2)

A.   Any element that is a member of set B is also a member of set A.

B.   No element is a member of all three sets A, B, and C.

C.   Any element that is a member of set U is also a member of set B.

D.   None of the above statements is true.

Answer: D. None of the above statements is true.

Answer A is incorrect because not all members of set B are also in set A. Answer B is incorrect because there are elements that are members of all three sets A, B, and C. Answer C is incorrect because not all members of set U are members of set B. This leaves answer D.

41. Select the statement that is the negation of the statement, "If the weather is cold, then the soccer game will be played."
(Average Rigor) (Skill 10.2)

    A.   If the weather is not cold, then the soccer game will be played.

    B.   The weather is cold and the soccer game was not played.

    C.   If the soccer game is played, then the weather is not cold.

    D.   The weather is cold and the soccer game will be played.

Answer: A. If the weather is not cold, then the soccer game will be played.

Negation of "if p, then q" is "(not p) and q". The words *not cold* negate *is cold*. Option A negates the circumstances under which the game will be played.

42. Select the statement below that is NOT logically equivalent to "If Mary works late, then Bill will prepare lunch."
(Average Rigor) (Skill 10.2)

    A.   Bill prepares lunch or Mary does not work late.

    B.   If Bill does not prepare lunch, then Mary did not work late.

    C.   If Bill prepares lunch, then Mary works late.

    D.   Mary does not work late or Bill prepares lunch.

Answer: C. If Bill prepares lunch, then Mary works late.

The second statement must also be an *if-then* statement to be logically equivalent to the first. Use the Law of Contraposition: If p, then q—not q, so, therefore, not p.

43. Select the rule of logical equivalence that directly (in one step) transforms the statement (i) into statement (ii),

    i. Not all the students have books.
    ii. Some students do not have books.
    (Average Rigor) (Skill 10.2)

    A. "If *p*, then *q*" is equivalent to "if not *q*, then *p*."

    B. "Not all are *p*" is equivalent to "some are not *p*."

    C. "Not *q*" is equivalent to "*p*."

    D. "All are not *p*" is equivalent to "none are *p*."

Answer: B. "Not all are *p*" is equivalent to "some are not *p*."

Identify the quantifiers, *all* and *some*. The negation of "not all have" is "some do not have." *Not all* students *have* books; therefore, *some* students *do not* have books.

44. Given that:
    i. No athletes are weak.
    ii. All football players are athletes.

    Determine which conclusion can be logically deduced.
    (Average Rigor) (Skill 10.2)

    A. Some football players are weak.

    B. All football players are weak.

    C. No football player is weak.

    D. None of the above is true.

Answer: C. No football player is weak.

Use the Law of Syllogism: If *p*, then *q*.
                          If *q*, then *r*.
                          Therefore if *p*, then *r*.

In *if-then* form, this would be, "If you are an athlete, then you are not weak. If you are a football player, then you are an athlete." Clearly, if you are a football player, you are an athlete, which means you are also not weak.

45.   **All of the following arguments have true conclusions, but one of the arguments is not valid. Select the argument that is not valid. (Average Rigor) (Skill 10.2)**

A.   All sea stars are echinoderms and all echinoderms are marine; therefore, all sea stars are marine.

B.   All spiders are dangerous. The black widow is dangerous. Therefore, the black widow is a spider.

C.   All crocodiles are amphibians and all amphibians breathe by lungs, gill, or skin; therefore, all crocodiles breathe by lungs, gill, or skin.

D.   All kids have hats and all boys are kids; therefore, all boys have hats.

Answer: B. All spiders are dangerous. The black widow is dangerous. Therefore, the black widow is a spider.

Options A and C follow the Law of Syllogism (If p, then q—If q, then r—Therefore, if p, then r.). Option D follows the Law of Detachment. (If p, then q [premise 1] p, [premise 2]—Therefore, q.). Option B is invalid because its conclusion does not follow from the premises.

In *if-then* form, these would be:

  If it's a spider, it's dangerous.
  If it's a black widow, it's dangerous.

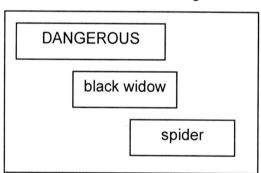

A black widow is dangerous, but it may or may not be a spider.

46. **Study the information given below. If a logical conclusion is given, select that conclusion.**

    Bob eats donuts or he eats yogurt. If Bob eats yogurt, then he is healthy. If Bob is healthy, then he can run the marathon. Bob does not eat yogurt.
    (Average Rigor) (Skill 10.2)

    A.   Bob does not eat donuts.

    B.   Bob is healthy.

    C.   If Bob runs the marathon, then he eats yogurt.

    D.   None of the above is warranted.

Answer: D. None of the above is warranted.

Use Disjunctive Syllogism: p or q
                            not p
                            Therefore, q

The fact that Bob does not eat yogurt means that he eats donuts. Because he eats donuts, Option A is incorrect. In addition, Bob is not healthy or running a marathon because he would have to eat yogurt for these things to happen.

47. **A restaurant employs 465 people. There are 280 waiters and 185 cooks. If 168 waiters and 85 cooks receive pay raises, what percent of the waiters will receive a pay raise?**
    (Average Rigor) (Skill 10.3)

    A.   36.13%

    B.   60%

    C.   60.22%

    D.   40%

Answer: B. 60%

The total number of waiters is 280 and only 168 of them get a pay raise. Divide the number getting a raise by the total number of waiters to get the percent.

$$\frac{168}{280} = 0.6 = 60\%.$$

48. Given the formula *d =rt*, (where *d* = distance, *r* = rate, and *t* = time), calculate the time required for a vehicle to travel 585 miles at a rate of 65 miles per hour.
(Average Rigor) (Skill 10.3)

   A.   8.5 hours

   B.   6.5 hours

   C.   9.5 hours

   D.   9 hours

Answer: D. 9 hours

We are given *d* = 585 miles and *r* = 65 miles per hour and *d =rt*. Solve for *t*.
$585 = 65t \rightarrow t = 9$ hours.

49. The price of gas was $3.27 per gallon. Your tank holds 15 gallons of fuel. You are using two tanks a week. How much will you save weekly if the price of gas goes down to $2.30 per gallon?
(Average Rigor) (Skill 10.3)

   A. $26.00

   B. $29.00

   C. $15.00

   D. $17.00

Answer: B. $29.00

15 gallons x 2 tanks = 30 gallons a week
30 gallons x $3.27 = $98.10
30 gallons x $2.30 = $69.00
$98.10 – $69.00 = $29.10 is approximately $29.00.

50. It takes five equally skilled people 9 hours to shingle Mr. Joe's roof. Let *t* be the time required for only three of these men to do the same job. Select the correct statement of the given condition.
(Rigorous) (Skill 10.3)

A. $\dfrac{3}{5} = \dfrac{9}{t}$

B. $\dfrac{9}{5} = \dfrac{3}{t}$

C. $\dfrac{5}{9} = \dfrac{3}{t}$

D. $\dfrac{14}{9} = \dfrac{t}{5}$

Answer: B. $\dfrac{9}{5} = \dfrac{3}{t}$

$$\frac{9 \text{ hours}}{5 \text{ people}} = \frac{3 \text{ people}}{t \text{ hours}}$$

51. In a sample of 40 full-time employees at a particular company, 35 were also holding down a part-time job requiring at least 10 hours/week. If this proportion holds for the entire company of 25,000 employees, how many full-time employees at this company are actually holding down a part-time job of at least 10 hours per week?
(Rigorous) (Skill 10.3)

A. 714

B. 625

C. 21,875

D. 28,571

Answer: C. 21,875

$\dfrac{35}{40}$ full-time employees have a part-time job also. Out of 25,000 full-time employees, the number that have a part-time job also is

$\dfrac{35}{40} = \dfrac{x}{25000} \rightarrow 40x = 875000 \rightarrow x = 21875$, so 21,875 full-time employees also have a part time job.

52. For each of the statements below, determine whether $x = \dfrac{1}{6}$ is a solution.

    i. $6x \le 4x^2 + 2$

    ii. $10x + 1 = 3(4x - 3)$

    iii. $|x - 1| = x$

    (Rigorous) (Skill 10.5)

    A.   i, ii, and iii

    B.   i and iii only

    C.   i only

    D.   iii only

Answer: C. i only

Substitute $x = \dfrac{1}{6}$ into each equation and solve.

i. $6\left(\dfrac{1}{6}\right) \le 4\left(\dfrac{1}{6}\right)^2 + 2 = 1 \le 4\left(\dfrac{1}{36}\right) + 2 \to 1 \le \dfrac{1}{9} + 2 \to 1 \le 2\dfrac{1}{9}$ True.

ii. $10\left(\dfrac{1}{6}\right) + 1 = 3\left(4\left(\dfrac{1}{6}\right) - 3\right) = 2\dfrac{2}{3} = 3\left(\dfrac{2}{3} - 3\right) \to 2\dfrac{2}{3} = \dfrac{6}{3} - 9 \to 2\dfrac{2}{3} = {}^{-}7$ False.

iii. $\left|\dfrac{1}{6} - 1\right| = \dfrac{1}{6} \to \left|\dfrac{1}{6} - \dfrac{6}{6}\right| = \dfrac{1}{6} \to \left|\dfrac{{}^{-}5}{6}\right| = \dfrac{1}{6} \to \dfrac{5}{6} = \dfrac{1}{6}$ False.

So, only (i) is true, which is answer **C**.

53.   Given $f(x) = (x)^3 - 3(x)^2 + 5$, find $x = -2$.
       (Rigorous) (Skill 10.5)

      A.   15

      B.   −15

      C.   25

      D.   −25

Answer: B. −15

Substitute $x = -2$.

$f(-2) = (^-2)^3 - 3 \times (^-2)^2 + 5$

$f(-2) = ^- 8 - 3(4) + 5$

$f(-2) = ^- 8 - 12 + 5$

$f(-2) = ^- 15$

54.   Choose the equation that is equivalent to the following:
       (Rigorous) (Skill 10.5)

$$\frac{3x}{5} - 5 = 5x$$

      A. $3x - 25 = 25x$

      B. $x - \dfrac{25}{3} = 25x$

      C. $6x - 50 = 75x$

      D. $x + 25 = 25x$

Answer: A. 3x − 25 = 25x

A is the correct answer because it is the original equation multiplied by 5. The other choices alter the answer to the original equation.

55. What is the equation that expresses the relationship between x and y in the table below?
(Rigorous) (Skill 10.5)

x	y
−2	4
−1	2
0	−2
1	−5
2	−8

A. $y = -x - 2$

B. $y = -3x - 2$

C. $y = 3x - 2$

D. $y = \dfrac{1}{3}x - 1$

Answer: B. y = −3x − 2

Solve by plugging in the values of x and y into the equations to see if they work. The answer is B because it is the only equation for which the values of x and y are correct.

56.   The figure below shows a running track in the shape of a rectangle with semicircles at each end.
        (Rigorous) (Skill 10.6)

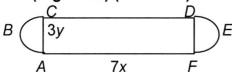

        Calculate the distance around the track.

        A. $6\pi y + 14x$

        B. $3\pi y + 7x$

        C. $6\pi y + 7x$

        D. $3\pi y + 14x$

Answer: D. $3\pi y + 14x$

The two semicircles of the track create one circle with a diameter 3y. The circumference of a circle is $C = \pi d$ so $C = 3\pi y$. The length of both sides of the track is 7x on each side, so the total circumference around the track is $3\pi y + 7x + 7x = 3\pi y + 14x$.

57.   **Choose the statement that is true for all real numbers.**
        (Rigorous) (Skill 10.6)

        A. $a = 0, b \neq 0$, then $\dfrac{b}{a}$ = undefined.

        B. $^-(a + (^-a)) = 2a$

        C. $2(ab) = ^-(2a)b$

        D. $^-a(b + 1) = ab - a$

Answer: A. $a = 0, b \neq 0$, then $\dfrac{b}{a}$ = undefined.

Any number divided by 0 is undefined.

58. Solve for x. $3x - \dfrac{2}{3} = \dfrac{5x}{2} + 2$

(Rigorous) (Skill 10.6)

A. $5\dfrac{1}{3}$

B. $\dfrac{17}{3}$

C. 2

D. $\dfrac{16}{2}$

Answer: A. $5\dfrac{1}{3}$

$3x(6) - \dfrac{2}{3}(6) = \dfrac{5x}{2}(6) + 2(6)$ 6 is the LCD of 2 and 3

$18x - 4 = 15x + 12$

$18x = 15x + 16$

$3x = 16$

$x = \dfrac{16}{3} = 5\dfrac{1}{3}$

59. **A car gets 25.36 miles per gallon. The car has been driven 83,310 miles. What is a reasonable estimate for the number of gallons of gas used?**
(Average Rigor) (Skill 10.7)

    A.   2,087 gallons

    B.   3,000 gallons

    C.   1,800 gallons

    D.   164 gallons

Answer: B. 3,000 gallons

Divide the number of miles by the miles per gallon to determine the approximate number of gallons of gas used. $\frac{83310 \text{ miles}}{25.36 \text{ miles per gallon}} = 3285$ gallons. This is approximately 3000 gallons.

60. **Round $1\frac{13}{16}$ of an inch to the nearest quarter of an inch.**
(Easy) (Skill 10.7)

    A. $1\frac{1}{4}$ inch

    B. $1\frac{5}{8}$ inch

    C. $1\frac{3}{4}$ inch

    D.   2 inches

Answer: C. $1\frac{3}{4}$ inch

$1\frac{13}{16}$ inches is approximately $1\frac{12}{16}$, which is also $1\frac{3}{4}$, which is the nearest $\frac{1}{4}$ of an inch, so the answer is C.

COMPETENCY 11.0   RECOGNIZE UNITY, FOCUS AND DEVELOPMENT IN WRITING

Skill 11.1   Recognize unnecessary shifts in point of view or distracting details that impair the development of the main idea in a piece of writing

Point of view defines the focus a writer assumes in relation to a given topic. It is extremely important to maintain a consistent point of view in order to create coherent paragraphs. Point of view is related to matters of person, tense, tone, and number.

Person — A shift in the form which indicates whether a person is speaking (first), is being spoken to (second), or is being spoken about (third) can disrupt continuity of a passage. In your essay, it is recommended that you write in the third person, as it is often considered the most formal of the modes of person. If you do decide to use the more informal first or second person (I, you, we) in your essay, be careful not to shift between first, second, and third persons from sentence to sentence or paragraph to paragraph.

Tense — Verb tenses indicate the time of an action or state of being—the past, present or future. It is important to stick largely to a selected tense, though this may not always be the case. For instance in an essay about the history of environmental protection, it might be necessary to include a paragraph about the future benefits or consequences of protecting the earth.

Tone — The tone of an essay varies greatly with the purpose, subject, and audience. It is best to assume a formal tone for this essay. (See Domain II, Skill 2.3.)

Number — Words change when their meanings are singular or plural. Make sure that you do not shift number needlessly; if a meaning is singular in one sentence, do not make it plural in the subsequent sentence.

Skill 11.2   Recognize revisions that improve the unity and focus of a piece of writing

Techniques to Maintain Focus

- **Focus on a main point.** The point should be clear to readers, and all sentences in the paragraph should relate to it.

- **Start the paragraph with a topic sentence.** This should be a general, one-sentence summary of the paragraph's main point, relating both back towards the thesis and toward the content of the paragraph. (A topic sentence is sometimes unnecessary if the paragraph continues a developing idea clearly introduced in a preceding paragraph, or if the paragraph appears in a narrative of events, where generalizations might interrupt the flow of the story.)

- **Stick to the point.** Eliminate sentences that do not support the topic sentence.

Be flexible. If there is not enough evidence to support the claim your topic sentence is making, do not fall into the trap of wandering or introducing new ideas within the paragraph. Either find more evidence, or adjust the topic sentence to collaborate with the available evidence.

Skill 11.3   Recognize thesis statements, topic sentences, and supporting elements

See Competency 1.0

COMPETENCY 12.0   RECOGNIZE EFFECTIVE ORGANIZATION IN WRITING

Skill 12.1   Recognize methods of paragraph organization

The **organization** of a written work includes two factors: the order in which the writer has chosen to present the different parts of the discussion or argument, and the relationships he or she constructs between these parts.

Written ideas need to be presented in a **logical order** so that a reader can follow the information easily and quickly. There are many different ways in which to order a series of ideas but they all share one thing in common: to lead the reader along a desired path while avoiding backtracking and skipping around in order to give a clear, strong presentation of the writer's main idea. *Some* of the ways in which a paragraph may be organized:

Sequence of events — In this type of organization, the details are presented in the order in which they have occurred. Paragraphs that describe a process or procedure, give directions, or outline a given period (such as a day or a month) are often arranged chronologically.

Statement support — In this type of organization, the main idea is stated and the rest of the paragraph explains or proves it. This is also referred to as relative or order of importance. This type of order is organized in four ways: most to least, least to most, most-least-most, and least-most-least.

Comparison-Contrast — In this type of organization, the compare-contrast pattern is used when a paragraph describes the differences or similarities of two or more ideas, actions, events, or things. Usually the topic sentence describes the basic relationship between the ideas or items and the rest of the paragraph explains this relationship.

Classification — In this type of organization, the paragraph presents grouped information about a topic. The topic sentence usually states the general category and the rest of the sentences show how various elements of the category have a common base and how they differ from the common base.

Cause and Effect — This pattern describes how two or more events are connected. The main sentence usually states the primary cause(s), the primary effect(s), and their connections. The rest of the sentences explain the connection—how one event caused the next.

Spatial/Place — In this type of organization, certain descriptions are organized according to the location of items in relation to each other and to a larger context. The orderly arrangement guides the reader's eye as he or she mentally envisions the scene or place being described.

Example, Clarification, and Definition — These types of organizations show, explain, or elaborate on the main idea. This can be done by showing specific cases, examining meaning multiple times, or extensive description of one term.

Skill 12.2 Recognize the use of transitional words or phrases

Even if the sentences that make up a given paragraph or passage are arranged in logical order, the document as a whole can still seem choppy, the various ideas disconnected. **Transitions**, words that signal relationships between ideas, can help improve the flow of a document. Transitions can help achieve clear and effective presentation of information by establishing connections between sentences, paragraphs, and sections of a document. With transitions, each sentence builds on the ideas in the last, and each paragraph has clear links to the preceding one. As a result, the reader receives clear directions on how to piece together the writer's ideas in a logically coherent argument. By signaling how to organize, interpret, and react to information, transitions allow a writer to explain their ideas effectively and elegantly.

Common Transitions

Logical Relationship	Transitional Expression
Similarity	also, in the same way, just as ... so too, likewise, similarly
Exception/Contrast	but, however, in spite of, on the one hand ... on the other hand, nevertheless, nonetheless, notwithstanding, in contrast, on the contrary, still, yet, although
Sequence/Order	first, second, third, ... next, then, finally, until
Time	after, afterward, at last, before, currently, during, earlier, immediately, later, meanwhile, now, presently, recently, simultaneously, since, subsequently, then
Example	for example, for instance, namely, specifically, to illustrate
Emphasis	even, indeed, in fact, of course, truly
Place/Position	above, adjacent, below, beyond, here, in front, in back, nearby, there
Cause and Effect	accordingly, consequently, hence, so, therefore, thus, as a result, because, consequently, hence, if...then, in short
Additional Support or Evidence	additionally, again, also, and, as well, besides, equally important, further, furthermore, in addition, moreover, then
Conclusion/Summary	finally, in a word, in brief, in conclusion, in the end, in the final analysis, on the whole, thus, to conclude, to summarize, in sum, in summary

Statement support	Most important, more significant, primarily, most essential
Addition	Again, also, and, besides, equally important, finally, furthermore, in addition, last, likewise, moreover, too
Clarification	Actually, clearly, evidently, in fact, in other words, obviously, of course, indeed

The following example shows good logical order and transitions

No one really knows how Valentine's Day started. There are several legends, however, which are often told. The first attributes Valentine's Day to a Christian priest who lived in Rome during the third century under the rule of Emperor Claudius. Rome was at war, and apparently, Claudius felt that married men did not fight as well as bachelors. Consequently, Claudius banned marriage for the duration of the war. However, Valentinus, the priest, risked his life to marry couples secretly in violation of Claudius' law. The second legend is even more romantic. In this story, Valentinus is a prisoner, having been condemned to death for refusing to worship pagan deities. While in jail, he fell in love with his jailer's daughter, who happened to be blind. Daily, he prayed for her sight to return, and miraculously it did. On February 14, the day that he was condemned to die, he was allowed to write the young woman a note. In this farewell letter, he promised eternal love and signed at the bottom of the page the now famous words, "Your Valentine."

Skill 12.3   Reorganize sentences to improve cohesion and the effective sequence of ideas

Techniques for revising written texts to achieve clarity and economy of expression

Enhancing Interest:

- Start out with an attention-grabbing introduction. This sets an engaging tone for the entire piece and it will be more likely to pull in the reader.
- Use dynamic vocabulary and varied sentence beginnings. Keep the reader on their toes. If they can predict what you are going to say next, switch it up.
- Avoid using clichés (as cold as ice, the best thing since sliced bread, nip it in the bud). These are easy shortcuts, but they are not interesting, memorable, or convincing.

Ensuring Understanding:

- Avoid using the words, "clearly," "obviously," and "undoubtedly." Often, things that are clear or obvious to the author are not as apparent to the reader. Instead of using these words, make your point so strongly that it is clear on its own.
- Use the word that best fits the meaning you intend for, even if it is longer or a little less common. Try to find a balance and go with a familiar yet precise word.
- When in doubt, explain further.

Revision of sentences to eliminate wordiness, ambiguity, and redundancy

Sometimes, students see this exercise as simply catching errors in spelling or word use. Students need to reframe their thinking about revising and editing. Some questions that need to be asked:

- Is the reasoning coherent?
- Is the point established?
- Does the introduction make the reader want to read this discourse?
- What is the thesis? Is it proven?
- What is the purpose? Is it clear? Is it useful, valuable, or interesting?
- Is the style of writing so wordy that it exhausts the reader and interferes with engagement?
- Is the writing so spare that it is boring?
- Are the sentences too uniform in structure?
- Are there too many simple sentences?
- Are too many of the complex sentences the same structure?

- Are the compounds truly compounds or are they unbalanced?
- Are parallel structures truly parallel?
- If there are characters, are they believable?
- If there is dialogue, is it natural or stilted?
- Is the title appropriate?
- Does the writing show creativity, or is it boring?
- Is the language appropriate? Is it too formal? Too informal? If jargon is used, is it appropriate?

Studies have clearly demonstrated that the most fertile area in teaching writing is this one. If students can learn to revise their own work effectively, they are well on their way to becoming effective, mature writers. Word processing is an important tool for teaching this stage in the writing process. Microsoft Word has tracking features that make the revision exchanges between teachers and students more effective than ever before.

COMPETENCY 13.0   RECOGNIZE EFFECTIVE SENTENCES

Skill 13.1   Recognize redundancy

Recognition of syntactical redundancy or omission

These errors occur when superfluous words have been added to a sentence or key words have been omitted from a sentence.

Redundancy

Incorrect: Joyce made sure that when her plane arrived that she retrieved all of her luggage.
Correct: Joyce made sure that when her plane arrived, she retrieved all of her luggage.

Incorrect: He was a mere skeleton of his former self.
Correct: He was a skeleton of his former self.

Omission

Incorrect: Dot opened her book, recited her textbook, and answered the teacher's subsequent question.
Correct: Dot opened her book, recited from the textbook, and answered the teacher's subsequent question.

Skill 13.2   Identify structures (e.g., sentences, fragments, run-on sentences)

Sentence structure

Recognize simple, compound, complex, and compound-complex sentences. Use dependent (subordinate) and independent clauses correctly to create these sentence structures.

Simple — Consists of one independent clause

Joyce wrote a letter.

Compound — Consists of two or more independent clauses. The two clauses are usually connected by a coordinating conjunction (and, but, or, nor, for, so, yet). Semicolons sometimes connect compound sentences.

Joyce wrote a letter, and Dot drew a picture.

Complex — Consists of an independent clause plus one or more dependent clauses. The dependent clause may precede the independent clause or follow it.

While Joyce wrote a letter, Dot drew a picture.

Compound/Complex — Consists of one or more dependent clauses plus two or more independent clauses.

When Mother asked the girls to demonstrate their newfound skills, Joyce wrote a letter, and Dot drew a picture.

Note: Do **not** confuse compound sentence elements with compound sentences.

Simple sentence with compound subject

<u>Joyce</u> and <u>Dot</u> wrote letters.
The <u>girl</u> in row three and the <u>boy</u> next to her were passing notes across the aisle.

Simple sentence with compound predicate

Joyce <u>wrote letters</u> and <u>drew pictures</u>.
The captain of the high school debate team <u>graduated with honors</u> and <u>studied broadcast journalism in college</u>.

Simple sentence with compound object of preposition

Coleen graded the students' essays for <u>style</u> and <u>mechanical accuracy</u>.

Types of Clauses

Clauses are connected word groups that are composed of *at least* one subject and one verb. (A subject is the doer of an action or the element that is being joined. A verb conveys either the action or the link.)

Students are waiting for the start of the assembly.
Subject   Verb

At the end of the play, students wait for the curtain to come down.
                    Subject Verb

Clauses can be independent or dependent.

Independent clauses can stand alone or they can be joined to other clauses.

Independent clause	for and nor	
Independent clause,	but or yet so	Independent clause
Independent clause	;	Independent clause
Dependent clause	,	Independent clause
Independent clause		Dependent clause

Dependent clauses, by definition, contain at least one subject and one verb. However, they cannot stand alone as complete sentences. They are structurally dependent on the main clause.

There are two types of dependent clauses: (1) those with a subordinating conjunction, and (2) those with a relative pronoun.

Sample coordinating conjunctions:
Although
When
If
Unless

Because

Unless a cure is discovered, many more people will die of the disease.
      Dependent clause   +   Independent clause

Sample relative pronouns:
Who
Whom
Which
That

The White House has an official website, which contains press releases, news updates, and biographies of the president and vice president.
(Independent clause + relative pronoun + relative dependent clause)

Fragments
Fragments occur (1) if word groups standing alone are missing either a subject or a verb, and (2) if word groups containing a subject and verb and standing alone are actually made dependent because of the use of subordinating conjunctions or relative pronouns.

Error: The teacher waiting for the class to complete the assignment.

Problem: This sentence is not complete because an -ing word alone does not function as a verb. When a helping verb is added (for example, was waiting), it will become a sentence.

Correction: *The teacher was waiting for the class to complete the assignment.*

Error: Until the last toy was removed from the floor.

Problem: Words such as *until, because, although, when,* and *if* make a clause dependent and thus incapable of standing alone. An independent clause must be added to make the sentence complete.

Correction: *Until the last toy was removed from the floor, the kids could not go outside to play.*

Error: The city will close the public library. Because of a shortage of funds.

Problem: The problem is the same as above. The dependent clause must be joined to the independent clause.

Correction: *The city will close the public library because of a shortage of funds.*

Fragments are tested in sentences tied to a passage. Items will be in one of two formats.

FORMAT A

Forensics experts conclude that the residents died from chemical <u>radiation. Or</u> perhaps from a mixture of toxic substances and asphyxiation.

A) radiation; or
B) radiation or
C) radiation or,
D) No change is necessary

FORMAT B

<u>Forensics</u> experts conclude that the residents died from chemical <u>radiation. Or</u> perhaps from a mixture of toxic substances and <u>asphyxiation</u>.

A) Forensics
B) radiation or
C) asphyxiation
D) No change is necessary

In each case, you must consider the punctuation between *radiation* and *or*. The punctuation decision is difficult if you do not understand that the second group of words, the one that begins with *Or*, is not a sentence. While these questions may appear to be only about punctuation, they are also about fragments.

The answer in both formats is B. The word group *Or perhaps from a mixture of toxic substances and asphyxiation* lacks a subject and a complete verb. It must be joined to the preceding sentence. A comma is not necessary since the word residents is the subject of the verb phrase *died from chemical radiation and of asphyxiation*.

PRACTICE EXERCISE — FRAGMENTS

Choose the option that corrects the underlined portion(s) of the sentence.
If no error exists, choose "No change is necessary."

1)   Despite the lack of funds in the <u>budget it</u> was necessary to rebuild the
        roads that were damaged from the recent floods.

        A) budget: it
        B) budget, it
        C) budget; it
        D) No change is necessary

2)   After determining that the fire was caused by faulty <u>wiring, the</u>
        building inspector said the construction company should be fined.

        A) wiring. The
        B) wiring the
        C) wiring; the
        D) No change is necessary

3)   Many years after buying a grand <u>piano Henry</u> decided he'd rather play
        the violin instead.

        A) piano: Henry
        B) piano, Henry
        C) piano; Henry
        D) No change is necessary

4)   Computers are being used more and more <u>frequently. because</u> of
        their capacity to store information.

        A) frequently because
        B) frequently, because
        C) frequently; because
        D) No change is necessary

5)   Doug washed the floors <u>every day. to</u> keep them clean for the
        guests.

        A) every day to
        B) every day,
        C) every day;
        D) No change is necessary.

ANSWER KEY: PRACTICE EXERCISE FOR FRAGMENTS

1. B   The clause that begins with *despite* is independent and must be separated with the clause that follows by a comma. Option A is incorrect because a colon is used to set off a list or to emphasize what follows. In Option B, a comma incorrectly suggests that the two clauses are dependent.

2. D   In the test item, a comma correctly separates the dependent clause *After...wiring* at the beginning of the sentence from the independent clause that follows. Option A incorrectly breaks the two clauses into separate sentences, while Option B omits the comma, and Option C incorrectly suggests that the phrase is an independent clause.

3. B   The *phrase Henry decided...instead* must be joined to the independent clause. Option A incorrectly puts a colon before *Henry decided*, and Option C incorrectly separates the phrase as if it was an independent clause.

4. A   The second clause *because...information* is dependent and must be joined to the first independent clause. Option B is incorrect because as the dependent clause comes at the end of the sentence, rather than at the beginning, a comma is not necessary. In Option C, a semi-colon incorrectly suggests that the two clauses are independent.

5. A   The second clause *to keep...guests* is dependent and must be joined to the first independent clause. Option B is incorrect because as the dependent clause comes at the end of the sentence, rather than at the beginning, a comma is not necessary. In Option C, a semi-colon incorrectly suggests that the two clauses are independent.

Run-on sentences and comma splices

Comma splices appear when two sentences are joined by only a comma. Fused sentences appear when two sentences run together with no punctuation at all.

Error: Dr. Sanders is a brilliant scientist, his research on genetic disorders won him a Nobel Prize.

Problem: A comma alone cannot join two independent clauses (complete sentences). The two clauses can be joined by a semi-colon, or they can be separated by a period.

Correction: *Dr. Sanders is a brilliant scientist; his research on genetic disorders won him a Nobel Prize.*
OR

Dr. Sanders is a brilliant scientist. His research on genetic disorders won him a Nobel Prize.

Error: Florida is noted for its beaches they are long, sandy, and beautiful.

Problem: The first sentence ends with the word *beaches*, and the second sentence cannot be joined with the first. The fused sentence error can be corrected in several ways: (1) one clause may be made dependent on another with a subordinating conjunction or a relative pronoun, (2) a semi-colon may be used to combine two equally important ideas, (3) the two independent clauses may be separated by a period.

Correction: *Florida is noted for its beaches, which are long, sandy, and beautiful.*
OR

Florida is noted for its beaches; they are long, sandy, and beautiful.
OR

Florida is noted for its beaches. They are long, sandy, and beautiful.

Error: The number of hotels has increased, however, the number of visitors has grown also.

Problem: The first sentence ends with the word *increased*, and a comma is not strong enough to connect it to the second sentence. The adverbial transition, however, does not function the same way as a coordinating conjunction and cannot be used with commas to link two sentences. Several different corrections are available.

Correction: *The number of hotels has increased; however, the number of visitors has grown also.*
[Two separate but closely related sentences are created with the use of the semicolon.]

OR

The number of hotels has increased. However, the number of visitors has grown also.
[Two separate sentences are created.]

OR

Although the number of hotels has increased, the number of visitors has grown also.
[One idea is made subordinate to the other and separated with a comma.]

OR

The number of hotels has increased, but the number of visitors has grown also.
[The comma before the coordinating conjunction *but* is appropriate. The adverbial transition, however, does not function the same way as the coordinating conjunction *but* does.]

PRACTICE EXERCISE — FUSED SENTENCES AND COMMA SPLICES

Choose the option that corrects an error in the underlined portion(s). If no error exists, choose "No change is necessary."

1)   Scientists are excited at the ability to clone a <u>sheep; however,</u> it is not yet known if the same can be done to humans.

       A) sheep, however,
       B) sheep. However,
       C) sheep, however;
       D) No change is necessary

2)   Because of the rising cost of college <u>tuition the</u> federal government now offers special financial assistance, <u>such as loans,</u> to students.

       A) tuition, the
       B) tuition; the
       C) such as loans
       D) No change is necessary

3)   As the number of homeless people continues to <u>rise, the major cities</u> such as <u>New York and Chicago,</u> are now investing millions of dollars in low-income housing.

       A) rise. The major cities
       B) rise; the major cities
       C) New York and Chicago
       D) No change is necessary

4)   Unlike in <u>the 1950s, most</u> households find the husband and wife working full-time to make <u>ends meet in many</u> different career fields.

       A) the 1950s; most
       B) the 1950s most
       C) ends meet, in many
       D) No change is necessary

ANSWER KEY: PRACTICE EXERCISE FOR COMMA SPLICES AND FUSED SENTENCES

1) B   Option B correctly separates two independent clauses. The comma in Option A after the word *sheep* creates a run-on sentence. The semi-colon in Option C does not separate the two clauses but occurs at an inappropriate point.

2) A   The comma in Option A correctly separates the independent clause and the dependent clause. The semi-colon in Option B is incorrect because one of the clauses is independent. Option C requires a comma to prevent a run-on sentence.

3) C   Option C is correct because a comma creates a run-on. Option A is incorrect because the first clause is dependent. The semi-colon in Option B incorrectly divides the dependent clause from the independent clause.

4) D   Option D correctly separates the two clauses with a comma. Option A incorrectly uses a semi-colon to divide the clauses. The lack of a comma in Option B creates a run-on sentence. Option C puts a comma in an inappropriate place.

Skill 13.3   Identify standard subject-verb agreement

A verb must correspond in the singular or plural form with the simple subject; it is not affected by any interfering elements. Note: A simple subject is never found in a prepositional phrase (a phrase beginning with a word such as *of*, *by*, *over*, *through*, *until*).

Present Tense Verb Form

	Singular	Plural
1st person (talking about oneself)	I do	We do
2nd person (talking to another)	You do	You do
3rd person (talking about someone or something)	He She does It	They do

Error: Sally, as well as her sister, plan to go into nursing.

Problem: The subject in the sentence is *Sally* alone, not the word *sister*. Therefore, the verb must be singular.

Correction: *Sally, as well as her sister, plans to go into nursing.*

Error: There has been many car accidents lately on that street.

Problem: The subject *accidents* in this sentence is plural; the verb must be plural also—even though it comes before the subject.

Correction: *There have been many car accidents lately on that street.*

Error: Every one of us have a reason to attend the school musical.

Problem: The simple subject is the word *everyone*, not the *us* in the prepositional phrase. Therefore, the verb must be singular also.

Correction: *Every one of us has a reason to attend the school musical.*

Error: Either the police captain or his officers is going to the convention.

Problem: In either/or and neither/nor constructions, the verb agrees with the subject closer to it.

Correction: *Either the police captain or his officers are going to the convention.*

PRACTICE EXERCISE — SUBJECT-VERB AGREEMENT

Choose the option that corrects an error in the underlined portion(s).
If no error exists, choose "No change is necessary."

1) Every year, the store <u>stays</u> open late, when shoppers desperately <u>try</u> to purchase Christmas presents as they <u>prepare</u> for the holiday.

    A. stay
    B. tries
    C. prepared
    D. No change is necessary.

2) Paul McCartney, together with George Harrison and Ringo Starr, <u>sing</u> classic Beatles songs on a special greatest-hits CD.

    A. singing
    B. sings
    C. sung
    D. No change is necessary.

3) My friend's cocker spaniel, while <u>chasing</u> cats across the street, always <u>manages</u> to <u>knock</u> over the trash cans.

    A. chased
    B. manage
    C. knocks
    D. No change is necessary.

4) Some of the ice on the driveway <u>have melted.</u>

    A. having melted
    B. has melted
    C. has melt
    D. No change is necessary.

5) Neither the criminal forensics expert nor the DNA blood evidence <u>provided</u> enough support for that verdict.

    A. provides
    B. were providing
    C. are providing
    D. No change is necessary.

ANSWER KEY: PRACTICE EXERCISE FOR SUBJECT-VERB AGREEMENT

1) D   Option D is correct because *store* is third person singular and requires the third person singular verbs *stays*. Option B is incorrect because the plural noun *shoppers* requires a plural verb *try*. In Option C, there is no reason to shift to the past tense *prepared*.

2) B   Option B is correct because the subject, *Paul McCartney*, is singular and requires the singular verb *sings*. Option A is incorrect because the present participle *singing* does not stand alone as a verb. Option C is incorrect because the past participle *sung* alone cannot function as the verb in this sentence.

3) D   Option D is the correct answer because the subject *cocker spaniel* is singular and requires the singular verb *manages*. Options A, B, and C do not work structurally with the sentence.

4) B   The subject of the sentence is *some*, which requires a third person singular verb, *has melted*. Option A incorrectly uses the present participle *having*, which does not act as a helping verb. Option C does not work structurally with the sentence.

5) A   In Option A, the singular subject *evidence* is closer to the verb and thus requires the singular in the neither/nor construction. Both Options B and C are plural forms with the helping verb and the present participle.

Skill 13.4 Identify double negatives, parallel structure, and standard placement of modifiers

Positive	Negative

To Be

Positive	Negative
I <u>am</u> afraid of the dark.	I <u>am not</u> afraid of the dark. (<u>I'm not</u>)
You are going to the store.	You <u>are not</u> going to the store (you'<u>re not</u> / aren't)
They <u>were</u> pretty flowers.	They <u>were not</u> pretty flowers. (<u>weren't</u>)
I <u>was</u> enjoying my day off.	I <u>was not</u> enjoying my day off (<u>wasn't</u>)

Conditionals

Positive	Negative
Charlotte <u>will</u> arrive at 8.	Charlotte <u>will not</u> arrive at 8. (<u>won't arrive</u>)
Robert <u>can</u> run 26 miles.	Robert <u>cannot</u> run 26 miles (<u>can't run</u>)
I <u>could have</u> been great!	I <u>could not</u> have been great. (<u>couldn't have</u>)

Present simple

Positive	Negative
I <u>want</u> to go home.	I <u>do not</u> want to go home (<u>don't</u>)
Veronica <u>walks</u> too slowly.	Veronica <u>does not</u> walk too slowly. (<u>doesn't</u>)

Past Simple

Positive	Negative
I <u>skipped</u> rope daily.	I <u>did not</u> skip rope daily. (<u>didn't</u>)

Present Perfect

Positive	Negative
My mom <u>has</u> made my costume.	My mom <u>has not</u> made my costume. (<u>hasn't</u>)
The Thompsons <u>have</u> just bought a dog.	The Thompsons <u>have not</u> just bought a dog. (<u>haven't</u>)

Have Versus Have Got

Positive	Negative
I <u>have</u> 2 sisters.	I <u>don't</u> have two sisters.
I <u>have</u> got 2 sisters.	I <u>haven't</u> got two sisters.
Jeremy <u>has</u> school tomorrow.	Jeremy <u>doesn't</u> have school tomorrow.
Jeremy <u>has</u> got school tomorrow.	Jeremy <u>hasn't</u> got school tomorrow.

Common negative words include:

no, not, none, nothing, nowhere, neither, nobody, no one, hardly, scarcely, barely.

A **double negative** occurs when two forms of negation are used in the same sentence. In order to correct a double negative, one of the negative words should be removed.

Error:	I haven't got nothing.
Correction:	I haven't got anything. OR I have nothing.
Error:	Don't nobody leave until 7 o'clock.
Correction:	Do not leave until 7 o'clock. OR Nobody leave until 7 o'clock.

It is also incorrect to combine a negative with an adverb such as *barely*, *scarcely*, or *hardly*.

Error:	I can't barely stand it.
Correction:	I can't stand it. OR I can barely stand it.

Faulty parallelism

Two or more elements stated in a single clause should be expressed with the same (or parallel) structure (e.g., all adjectives, all verb forms, or all nouns).

Error: She needed to be beautiful, successful, and have fame.

Problem: The phrase to be is followed by two different structures: *beautiful* and *successful* are adjectives, and *have fame* is a verb phrase.

Correction: *She needed to be beautiful, successful, and famous.*
　　　　　　　(adjective) (adjective)　　(adjective)
　　　　　　　　　　　　OR
She needed beauty, success, and fame.
　　　　　(noun)　(noun)　　　(noun)

Error: I plan either to sell my car during the spring or during the summer.

Problem: Paired conjunctions (also called correlative conjunctions) such as *either-or, both-and, neither-nor, not only-but also* need to be followed with similar structures. In the sentence above, *either* is followed by *to sell my car during the spring,* while *or* is followed only by the phrase *during the summer.*

Correction: *I plan to sell my car during either the spring or the summer.*

Error: The President pledged to lower taxes and that he would cut spending to lower the national debt.

Problem: Since the phrase *to lower taxes* follows the verb *pledged,* a similar structure of *to* is needed with the phrase *cut spending.*

Correction: *The President pledged to lower taxes and to cut spending to lower the national debt.*
OR
The President pledged that he would lower taxes and cut spending to lower the national debt.

PRACTICE EXERCISE — PARALLELISM

Choose the sentence that expresses the thought most clearly and effectively and that has no error in structure.

1. A. Andy found the family tree, researches the Irish descendents, and he was compiling a book for everyone to read.

    B. Andy found the family tree, researched the Irish descendents, and compiled a book for everyone to read.

    C. Andy finds the family tree, researched the Irish descendents, and compiled a book for everyone to read.

2. A. In the last ten years, computer technology has advanced so quickly that workers have had difficulty keeping up with the new equipment and the increased number of functions.

    B. Computer technology has advanced so quickly in the last ten years that workers have had difficulty to keep up with the new equipment and by increasing number of functions.

    C. In the last ten years, computer technology has advanced so quickly that workers have had difficulty keeping up with the new equipment and the number of functions are increasing.

3. A. The Florida State History Museum contains exhibits honoring famous residents, a video presentation about the state's history, an art gallery featuring paintings and sculptures, and they even display a replica of the Florida Statehouse.

    B. The Florida State History Museum contains exhibits honoring famous residents, a video presentation about the state's history, an art gallery featuring paintings and sculptures, and even a replica of the Florida Statehouse.

    C. The Florida State History Museum contains exhibits honoring famous residents, a video presentation about the state's history, an art gallery featuring paintings and sculptures, and there is even a replica of the Florida Statehouse.

4.   A.   Either the criminal justice students had too much practical experience and limited academic preparation or too much academic preparation and little practical experience.

     B.   The criminal justice students either had too much practical experience and limited academic preparation or too much academic preparation and little practical experience.

     C.   The criminal justice students either had too much practical experience and limited academic preparation or had too much academic preparation and little practical experience.

5.   A.   Filmmaking is an arduous process in which the producer hires the cast and crew, chooses locations for filming, supervises the actual production, and guides the editing.

     B.   Because it is an arduous process, filmmaking requires the producer to hire a cast and crew and choose locations, supervise the actual production, and guides the editing.

     C.   Filmmaking is an arduous process in which the producer hires the cast and crew, chooses locations for filming, supervises the actual production, and guided the editing.

ANSWER KEY: PRACTICE EXERCISE FOR PARALLELISM

1. B   Option B uses parallelism by presenting a series of past tense verbs *found, researched*, and *compiled*. Option A interrupts the parallel structure of past tense verbs with *found, researches*, and *he was compiling*. Option C uses present tense verbs and then shifts to past tense with *finds, researched*, and *compiled*.

2. A   Option A uses parallel structure at the end of the sentence: *the new equipment and the increased number of functions*. Option B creates a faulty structure with *to keep up with the new equipment and by increasing number of functions*. Option C creates faulty parallelism with *the number of functions are increasing*.

3. B   Option B uses parallelism by presenting a series of noun phrases acting as objects of the verb *contains*. Option A interrupts that parallelism by inserting *they even display*, and Option C interrupts the parallelism with the addition of *there is*.

4. C   In the either-or parallel construction, look for a balance on both sides. Option C creates that balanced parallel structure—*either had...or had*. Options A and B do not create the balance. In Option A, the structure is *Either the students...or too much*. In Option B, the structure is *either had...or too much*.

5. A   Option A uses parallelism by presenting a series of verbs with objects: *hires the cast and crew, chooses locations for filming, supervises the actual production, and guides the editing*. The structure of Option B incorrectly suggests that filmmaking chooses locations, supervises the actual production, and guides the editing. Option C interrupts the series of present tense verbs by inserting the participle *guided*, instead of the present tense *guides*.

Modifiers

Particular phrases that are not placed near the one word they modify often result in misplaced modifiers. Particular phrases that do not relate to the subject being modified result in dangling modifiers.

Error: Weighing the options carefully, a decision was made regarding the punishment of the convicted murderer.

Problem: Who is weighing the options? No one capable of weighing is named in the sentence; thus, the participle phrase *weighing the options carefully* dangles. This problem can be corrected by adding a subject of the sentence capable of doing the action.

Correction: *Weighing the options carefully, the judge made a decision regarding the punishment of the convicted murderer.*

Error: Returning to my favorite watering hole brought back many fond memories.

Problem: The person who returned is never indicated, and the participle phrase dangles. This problem can be corrected by creating a dependent clause from the modifying phrase.

Correction: *When I returned to my favorite watering hole, many fond memories came back to me.*

Error: One damaged house stood only to remind townspeople of the hurricane.

Problem: The placement of the misplaced modifier only suggests that the sole reason the house remained was to serve as a reminder. The faulty modifier creates ambiguity.

Correction: *Only one damaged house stood, reminding townspeople of the hurricane.*

Error: Recovered from the five-mile hike, the obstacle course was a piece of cake for the Boy Scout troop.

Problem: The obstacle course is not recovered from the five-mile hike, so the modifying phrase must be placed closer to the word, *troop*, that it modifies.

Correction: *The obstacle course was a piece of cake for the Boy Scout troop, which had just recovered from a five-mile hike.*

PRACTICE EXERCISE — MISPLACED AND DANGLING MODIFIERS

Choose the sentence that expresses the thought most clearly and effectively and that has no error in structure.

1) A. Attempting to remove the dog from the well, the paramedic tripped and fell in also.

   B. As the paramedic attempted to remove the dog from the well, he tripped and fell in also.

   C. The paramedic tripped and fell in also attempting to remove the dog from the well.

2) A. To save the wounded child, a powerful explosion ripped through the operating room as the doctors worked.

   B. In the operating room, as the wounded child was being saved, a powerful explosion ripped through.

   C. To save the wounded child, the doctors worked as an explosion ripped through the operating room.

3) A. One hot July morning, a herd of giraffes screamed wildly in the jungle next to the wildlife habitat.

   B. One hot July morning, a herd of giraffes screamed in the jungle wildly next to the wildlife habitat.

   C. One hot July morning, a herd of giraffes screamed in the jungle next to the wildlife habitat, wildly.

4) A. Looking through the file cabinets in the office, the photographs of the crime scene revealed a new suspect in the investigation.

   B. Looking through the file cabinets in the office, the detective discovered photographs of the crime scene which revealed a new suspect in the investigation.

   C. A new suspect in the investigation was revealed in photographs of the crime scene that were discovered while looking through the file cabinets in the office.

ANSWER KEY: PRACTICE EXERCISE FOR MISPLACED AND DANGLING MODIFIERS

1) B   Option B corrects the dangling participle *attempting to remove the dog from the well* by creating a dependent clause introducing the main clause. In Option A, the introductory participle phrase *Attempting...well* does not refer to a paramedic, the subject of the main clause. The word also in Option C incorrectly implies that the paramedic was doing something besides trying to remove the dog.

2) C   Option C corrects the dangling modifier *to save the wounded child* by adding the concrete subject *doctors worked*. Option A infers that an explosion was working to save the wounded child. Option B never tells who was trying to save the wounded child.

3) A   Option A places the adverb *wildly* closest to the verb screamed, which it modifies. Both Options B and C incorrectly place the modifier away from the verb.

4) B   Option B corrects the modifier *looking through the file cabinets in the office* by placing it next to the detective who is doing the looking. Option A sounds as though the photographs were looking; Option C has no one doing the looking.

COMPETENCY 14.0   RECOGNIZE STANDARD AMERICAN ENGLISH USAGE

Skill 14.1   Recognize the standard use of verb forms and cases

Past tense and past participles

Both regular and irregular verbs must appear in their standard forms for each tense. Note: the -ed or -d ending is added to regular verbs in the past tense and for past participles.

Infinitive	Past Tense	Past Participle
Bake	Baked	Baked

Irregular Verb Forms

Infinitive	Past Tense	Past Participle
Be	Was, were	Been
Become	Became	Become
Break	Broke	Broken
Bring	Brought	Brought
Choose	Chose	Chosen
Come	Came	Come
Do	Did	Done
Draw	Drew	Drawn
Eat	Ate	Eaten
Fall	Fell	Fallen
Forget	Forgot	Forgotten
Freeze	Froze	Frozen
Give	Gave	Given
Go	Went	Gone
Grow	Grew	Grown
Have/has	Had	Had
Hide	Hid	Hidden
Know	Knew	Known
Lay	Laid	Laid
Lie	Lay	Lain
Ride	Rode	Ridden
Rise	Rose	Risen
Run	Ran	Run
See	Saw	Seen
Steal	Stole	Stolen
Take	Took	Taken
Tell	Told	Told
Throw	Threw	Thrown
Wear	Wore	Worn
Write	Wrote	Written

Error: She should have went to her doctor's appointment at the scheduled time.

Problem: The past participle of the verb *to go* is *gone*. *Went* expresses the simple past tense.

Correction: *She should have gone to her doctor's appointment at the scheduled time.*

Error: My train is suppose to arrive before two o'clock.

Problem: The verb following *train* is a present tense passive Construction, which requires the present tense verb *to be* and the past participle.

Correction: *My train is supposed to arrive before two o'clock.*

Error: Linda should of known that the car wouldn't start after leaving it out in the cold all night.

Problem: *Should of* is a nonstandard expression. *Of is* not a verb.

Correction: *Linda should have known that the car wouldn't start after leaving it out in the cold all night.*

PRACTICE EXERCISE — STANDARD VERB FORMS

Choose the option that corrects an error in the underlined portion(s). If no error exists, choose "No change is necessary."

1)   My professor _had knew_ all along that we would pass his course.

      A. know
      B. had known
      C. knowing
      D. No change is necessary

2)   Kevin was asked to erase the vulgar words he _had wrote._

      A. writes
      B. has write
      C. had written
      D. No change is necessary

3)   Melanie _had forget_ to tell her parents that she left the cat in the closet.

      A. had forgotten
      B. forgot
      C. forget
      D. No change is necessary

4)   Craig always _leave_ the house a mess when his parents aren't there.

      A. left
      B. leaves
      C. leaving
      D. No change is necessary

5)   The store manager accused Kathy of _having stole_ more than five hundred dollars from the safe.

      A. has stolen
      B. having stolen
      C. stole
      D. No change is necessary

ANSWER KEY: PRACTICE EXERCISE FOR STANDARD VERB FORMS

1. B   Option B is correct because the past participle needs the helping verb *had*. Option A is incorrect because *it* is in the infinitive tense. Option C incorrectly uses the present participle.

2. C   Option C is correct because the past participle follows the helping verb *had*. Option A uses the verb in the present tense. Option B is an incorrect use of the verb.

3. A   Option A is correct because the past participle uses the helping verb *had*. Option B uses the wrong form of the verb. Option C uses the wrong form of the verb.

4. B   Option B correctly uses the past tense of the verb. Option A uses the verb in an incorrect way. Option C uses the verb without a helping verb like *is*.

5. B   Option B is correct because it is the past participle. Option A and C use the verb incorrectly.

Inappropriate shifts in verb tense

Verb tenses must refer to the same period consistently, unless a change in time is required.

Error: Despite the increased amount of students in the school this year, overall attendance is higher last year at the sporting events.

Problem: The verb *is* represents an inconsistent shift to the present tense when the action refers to a past occurrence.

Correction: *Despite the increased amount of students in the school this year, overall attendance was higher last year at sporting events.*

Error: My friend Lou, who just competed in the marathon, ran since he was twelve years old.

Problem: Because Lou continues to run, the present perfect tense is needed.

Correction: *My friend Lou, who just competed in the marathon, has ran since he was twelve years old.*

Error: The Mayor congratulated Wallace Mangham, who renovates the city hall last year.

Problem: Although the speaker is talking in the present, the action of renovating the city hall was in the past.

Correction: *The Mayor congratulated Wallace Mangham, who renovated the city hall last year.*

PRACTICE EXERCISE — SHIFTS IN TENSE

Choose the option that corrects an error in the underlined portion(s).
If no error exists, choose "No change is necessary."

1)   After we <u>washed</u> the fruit that had <u>growing</u> in the garden, we knew
       there <u>was</u> a store that would buy them.

       A) washing
       B) grown
       C) is
       D) No change is necessary.

2)   The tourists <u>used</u> to visit the Atlantic City boardwalk whenever they
       <u>vacationed</u> during the summer. Unfortunately, their numbers have
       <u>diminished</u> every year.

       A) use
       B) vacation
       C) diminish
       D) No change is necessary.

3)   When the temperature <u>drops</u> to below thirty-two degrees Fahrenheit,
       the water on the lake <u>freezes</u>, which <u>allowed</u> children to skate across it.

       A) dropped
       B) froze
       C) allows
       D) No change is necessary.

4)   The artists were <u>hired</u> to <u>create</u> a monument that would pay tribute to
       the men who were <u>killed</u> in World War Two.

       A) hiring
       B) created
       C) killing
       D) No change is necessary.

5)   Emergency medical personnel rushed to the scene of the shooting,
       where many injured people <u>waiting</u> for treatment.

       A) wait
       B) waited
       C) waits
       D) No change is necessary.

ANSWER KEY: PRACTICE EXERCISE FOR SHIFTS IN TENSE

1) B   The past participle *grown* is needed instead of *growing,* which is the progressive tense. Option A is incorrect because the past participle *washed* takes the *-ed.* Option C incorrectly replaces the past participle *was* with the present tense *is.*

2) D   Option A is incorrect because *use* is the present tense. Option B incorrectly uses the noun *vacation.* Option C incorrectly uses the present tense *diminish* instead of the past tense *diminished.*

3) C   The present tense *allows* is necessary in the context of the sentence. Option A is incorrect because *dropped* is a past participle. Option B is incorrect because *froze* is also a past participle.

4) D   Option A is incorrect because *hiring* is the present tense. Option B is incorrect because *created* is a past participle. In Option C, *killing* does not fit into the context of the sentence.

5) B   In Option B, *waited* corresponds with the past tense *rushed.* In Option A, *wait* is incorrect because it is present tense. In Option C, *waits* is incorrect because the noun *people* is plural and requires the singular form of the verb.

Skill 14.2 **Recognize the standard use of pronouns/antecedents and plural and possessive forms of nouns**

Agreements between pronoun and antecedent

A pronoun must correspond to its antecedent in number (singular or plural), person (first, second, or third person) and gender (male, female, or neutral). A pronoun must refer clearly to a single word, not to a complete idea.

A **pronoun shift** is a grammatical error in which the author starts a sentence, paragraph, or section of a paper using one particular type of pronoun and then suddenly shifts to another. This often confuses the reader.

Error: A teacher should treat all their students fairly.

Problem: Since *A teacher* is singular, the pronoun referring to it must also be singular. Otherwise, the noun has to be made plural.

Correction: *Teachers should treat all their students fairly.*

Error: When an actor is rehearsing for a play, it often helps if you can memorize the lines in advance.

Problem: *Actor* is a third-person word; that is, the writer is talking about the subject. The pronoun *you* is in the second person, which means the writer is talking to the subject.

Correction: *When actors are rehearsing for plays, it helps if they can memorize the lines in advance.*

Error: The workers in the factory were upset when his or her paychecks didn't arrive on time.

Problem: *Workers* is a plural form, while *his or her* refers to one person.

Correction: *The workers in the factory were upset when their paychecks didn't arrive on time.*

Error: The charity auction was highly successful, which pleased everyone.

Problem: In this sentence, the pronoun *which* refers to the idea of the auction's success. In fact, *which* has no antecedent in the sentence; the word *success* is not stated.

Correction: *Everyone was pleased with the success of the auction.*

Error: Lana told Melanie that she would like aerobics.

Problem: The person that she refers to is unclear; it could be either Lana or Melanie.

Correction: *Lana said that Melanie would like aerobics.*

OR

Lana told Melanie that she, Melanie, would like aerobics.

Error: I dislike accounting, even though my brother is one.

Problem: A person's occupation is not the same as a field, and the pronoun *one* is thus incorrect. Note that the word *accountant* is not used in the sentence, so *one* has no antecedent.

Correction: *I dislike accounting, even though my brother is an accountant.*

PRACTICE EXERCISE — PRONOUN/ANTECEDENT AGREEMENT

Choose the option that corrects an error in the underlined portion(s).
If no error exists, choose "No change is necessary."

1) <u>You</u> can get to Martha's Vineyard by driving from Boston to Woods Hole. Once there, you can travel over on a ship, but <u>you</u> may find traveling by <u>airplane</u> to be an exciting experience.

    A. They
    B. visitors
    C. it
    D. No change is necessary.

2) Both the city leader and the <u>journalist</u> are worried about the new interstate; <u>she fears</u> <u>the new roadway</u> will destroy precious farmland.

    A. journalist herself
    B. they fear
    C. it
    D. No change is necessary.

3) When <u>hunters</u> are looking for deer in <u>the woods, you</u> must remain quiet for long periods.

    A. they
    B. it
    C. we
    D. No change is necessary.

4) Florida's strong economy is based on the importance of the citrus industry. <u>Producing</u> orange juice for most of the country.

    A. They produce
    B. Who produce
    C. Farmers there produce
    D. No change is necessary.

5) Dr. Kennedy told Paul Elliot, <u>his</u> assistant, that <u>he</u> would have to finish grading the tests before going home, no matter how long <u>it</u> took.

    A. their
    B. he, Paul
    C. they
    D. No change is necessary.

ANSWER KEY: PRACTICE EXERCISE FOR PRONOUN AGREEMENT

1) D   Pronouns must be consistent. As *you* is used throughout the sentence, the shift to *visitors* is incorrect. Option A, *They*, is vague and unclear. Option C, *it*, is also unclear.

2) B   The plural pronoun *they* is necessary to agree with the two nouns *leader* and *journalist*. There is no need for the reflexive pronoun *herself* in Option A. Option C, *it*, is vague.

3) A   The shift to *you* is unnecessary. The plural pronoun *they* is necessary to agree with the noun *hunters*. The word *we* in Option C is vague; the reader does not know to whom the word *we* might refer. Option B, *it*, has no antecedent.

4) C   The noun *farmers* is needed for clarification because *producing* is vague. Option A is incorrect because *they produce* is vague. Option B is incorrect because *who* has no antecedent and creates a fragment.

5) B   The repetition of the name *Paul* is necessary to clarify to whom the pronoun *he* is referring. (It could be Dr. Kennedy.) Option A is incorrect because the singular pronoun *his* is needed, not the plural pronoun *their*. Option C is incorrect because the pronoun *it* refers to the plural noun *tests*.

Rule for clear pronoun references

Make sure that the antecedent reference is clear and cannot refer to something else
A "distant relative" is a relative pronoun or a relative clause that has been placed too far away from the antecedent to which it refers. It is a common error to place a verb between the relative pronoun and its antecedent.

Error: Return the books to the library that are overdue.

Problem: The relative clause "that are overdue" refers to the "books" and should be placed immediately after the antecedent.

Correction: Return the books that are overdue to the library.
           or
           Return the overdue books to the library.

A pronoun should not refer to adjectives or possessive nouns
Adjectives, nouns, or possessive pronouns should not be used as antecedents. This will create ambiguity in sentences.

Error: In Todd's letter, he told his mom he'd broken the priceless vase.

Problem: In this sentence, the pronoun *he* seems to refer to the noun phrase *Todd's letter* though it was probably meant to refer to the possessive noun *Todd's*.

Correction: In his letter, Todd told his mom that he had broken the priceless vase.

A pronoun should not refer to an implied idea
A pronoun must refer to a specific antecedent rather than an implied antecedent. When an antecedent is not stated specifically, the reader has to guess or assume the meaning of a sentence. Pronouns that do not have antecedents are called expletives. *It* and *there* are the most common expletives, though other pronouns can also become expletives as well. In informal conversation, expletives allow for casual presentation of ideas without supporting evidence. However, in writing that is more formal, it is best to be more precise.

Error: She said that it is important to floss every day.

Problem: The pronoun *it* refers to an implied idea.

Correction: She said that flossing every day is important.

Error: They returned the book because there were missing pages.

Problem: The pronouns *they* and *there* do not refer to the antecedent.

Correction: The customer returned the book with missing pages.

Using Who, That, and Which

Who, whom, and **whose** refer to human beings and can either introduce essential or nonessential clauses. **That** refers to things other than humans and it is used to introduce essential clauses. **Which** refers to things other than humans and is used to introduce nonessential clauses.

Error: The doctor that performed the surgery said the man would fully recover.

Problem: Since the relative pronoun is referring to a human, *who* should be used.

Correction: The doctor who performed the surgery said the man would fully recover.

Error: That ice cream cone that you just ate looked delicious.

Problem: *That* has already been used so you must use *which* to introduce the next clause, whether it is essential or nonessential.

Correction: That ice cream cone, which you just ate, looked delicious.

Proper case forms

Pronouns, unlike nouns, change case forms. Pronouns must be in the subjective, objective, or possessive form according to their function in the sentence.

Personal Pronouns

	Subjective (Nominative)		Possessive		Objective	
	Singular	Plural	Singular	Plural	Singular	Plural
1st person	I	We	My	Our	Me	Us
2nd person	You	You	Your	Your	You	You
3rd person	He She It	They	His Her Its	Their	Him Her It	them

Relative Pronouns

Who   Subjective/Nominative
Whom Objective
Whose Possessive

Error: Tom and me have reserved seats for next week's baseball game.

Problem: The pronoun *me* is the subject of the verb *have reserved* and should be in the subjective form.

Correction: *Tom and I have reserved seats for next week's baseball game.*

Error: Mr. Green showed all of we students how to make paper hats.

Problem: The pronoun *we* is the object of the preposition *of*. It should be in the objective form, *us*.

Correction: *Mr. Green showed all of us students how to make paper hats.*

Error: Who's coat is this?

Problem: The interrogative possessive pronoun is *whose*; *who's* is the contraction for who is.

Correction: *Whose coat is this?*

Error: The voters will choose the candidate whom has the best qualifications for the job.

Problem: The case of the relative pronoun *who* or *whom* is determined by the pronoun's function in the clause in which it appears. The word *who* is in the subjective case, and *whom* is in the objective. Analyze how the pronoun is being used within the sentence.

Correction: *The voters will choose the candidate who has the best qualifications for the job.*

PRACTICE EXERCISE — PRONOUN CASE

Choose the option that corrects an error in the underlined portion(s).
If no error exists, choose "No change is necessary."

1)   Even though Sheila and _he_ had planned to be alone at the diner,
     they were joined by three friends of _their's_ instead.

     A) him
     B) him and her
     C) theirs
     D) No change is necessary.

2)   Uncle Walter promised to give his car to _whomever_ will guarantee
     to drive it safely.

     A) whom
     B) whoever
     C) them
     D) No change is necessary.

3)   Eddie and _him_ gently laid _the body_ on the ground next to _the sign_.

     A) he
     B) them
     C) it
     D) No change is necessary.

4)   Mary, _who_ is competing in the chess tournament, is a better player
     than _me_.

     A) whose
     B) whom
     C) I
     D) No change is necessary.

5)   _We, ourselves,_ have decided not to buy property in that development;
     however, our friends have already bought _themselves_ some land.

     A) We, ourself,
     B) their selves
     C) their self
     D) No change is necessary.

ANSWER KEY: PRACTICE EXERCISE FOR PRONOUN CASE

1) C   The possessive pronoun *theirs* does not need an apostrophe. Option A is incorrect because the subjective pronoun *he* is needed in this sentence. Option B is incorrect because the subjective pronoun *they*, not the objective pronouns *him* and *her*, is needed.

2) B   The subjective case *whoever*—not the objective case *whomever*—is the subject of the relative clause *whoever will guarantee to drive it safely*. Option A is incorrect because *whom* is an objective pronoun. Option C is incorrect because *car* is singular and takes the pronoun *it*.

3) A   The subjective pronoun *he* is needed as the subject of the verb *laid*. Option B is incorrect because *them* is vague; the noun *body* is needed to clarify *it*. Option C is incorrect because *it* is vague, and the noun *sign* is necessary for clarification.

4) C   The subjective pronoun *I* is needed because the comparison is understood. Option A incorrectly uses the possessive *whose*. Option B is incorrect because the subjective pronoun *who*, and not the objective *whom*, is needed.

5) B   The reflexive pronoun *themselves* refers to the plural *friends*. Option A is incorrect because the plural *we* requires the reflexive *ourselves*. Option C is incorrect because the possessive pronoun *their* is never joined with either *self* or *selves*.

Skill 14.3 **Recognize the standard use and formations of adverbs and adjectives**

Correct use of adjectives and adverbs

Adjectives are words that modify or describe nouns or pronouns. Adjectives usually precede the words they modify, but not always; for example, an adjective occurs after a linking verb.

Adverbs are words that modify verbs, adjectives, or other adverbs. They cannot modify nouns. Adverbs answer such questions as how, why, when, where, how much, or how often something is done. Many adverbs are formed by adding -ly.

Error: The birthday cake tasted sweetly.

Problem: *Tasted* is a linking verb; the modifier that follows should be an adjective, not an adverb.

Correction: *The birthday cake tasted sweet.*

Error: You have done good with this project.

Problem: *Good* is an adjective and cannot be used to modify a verb phrase such as *have done.*

Correction: *You have done well with this project.*

Error: The coach was positive happy about the team's chance of winning.

Problem: The adjective *positive* cannot be used to modify another adjective, *happy.* An adverb is needed instead.

Correction: *The coach was positively happy about the team's chance of winning.*

Error: The fireman acted quick and brave to save the child from the burning building.

Problem: *Quick and brave* are adjectives and cannot be used to describe a verb. Adverbs are needed instead.

Correction: *The fireman acted quickly and bravely to save the child from the burning building.*

PRACTICE EXERCISE — ADJECTIVES AND ADVERBS

Choose the option that corrects an error in the underlined portion(s).
If no error exists, choose "No change is necessary."

1) Moving <u>quick</u> throughout the house, the burglar <u>removed</u> several priceless antiques before <u>carelessly</u> dropping his wallet.

   A) quickly
   B) remove
   C) careless
   D) No change is necessary.

2) The car <u>crashed loudly</u> into the retaining wall before spinning <u>wildly</u> on the sidewalk.

   A) crashes
   B) loudly
   C) wild
   D) No change is necessary.

3) The airplane <u>landed safe</u> on the runway after <u>nearly</u> colliding with a helicopter.

   A) land
   B) safely
   C) near
   D) No change is necessary.

4) The <u>horribly bad</u> special effects in the movie disappointed us <u>great</u>.

   A) horrible
   B) badly
   C) greatly
   D) No change is necessary.

5) The man promised to obey the rules of the social club <u>faithfully</u>.

   A) faithful
   B) faithfulness
   C) faith
   D) No change is necessary.

ANSWER KEY: PRACTICE EXERCISE FOR ADJECTIVES AND ADVERBS

1) A   The adverb *quickly* is needed to modify *moving*. Option B is incorrect because it uses the wrong form of the verb. Option C is incorrect because the adverb *carelessly* is needed before the verb *dropping,* not the adjective *careless.*

2) D   The sentence is correct as it is written. Adverbs *loudly* and *wildly* are needed to modify *crashed* and *spinning.* Option A incorrectly uses the verb *crashes* instead of the participle *crashing*, which acts as an adjective.

3) B   The adverb *safely* is needed to modify the verb *landed.* Option A is incorrect because *land* is a noun. Option C is incorrect because *near* is an adjective, not an adverb.

4) C   The adverb *greatly* is needed to modify the verb *disappointed.* Option A is incorrect because *horrible* is an adjective, not an adverb. Option B is incorrect because *bad* needs to modify the adverb *horribly.*

5) D   The adverb *faithfully* is the correct modifier of the verb *promised.* Option A is an adjective used to modify nouns. Neither Option B nor Option C, which are both nouns, is a modifier.

Appropriate comparative and superlative degree forms

When comparisons are made, the correct form of the adjective or adverb must be used. The comparative form is used for two items. The superlative form is used for more than two.

	Comparative	Superlative
slow	slower	slowest
young	younger	youngest
tall	taller	tallest

With some words, more and most are used to make comparisons instead of -er and -est.

quiet	more quiet	most quiet
energetic	more energetic	most energetic
quick	more quickly	most quickly

Comparisons must be made between similar structures or items. In the sentence, "My house is similar in color to Steve's," one house is being compared to another house as understood by the use of the possessive *Steve's*.

On the other hand, if the sentence reads "My house is similar in color to Steve," the comparison would be faulty because it would be comparing the house to Steve, not to Steve's house.

Error: Last year's rides at the carnival were bigger than this year.

Problem: In the sentence as it is worded above, the rides at the carnival are being compared to this year, not to this year's rides.

Correction: *Last year's rides at the carnival were bigger than this year's.*

PRACTICE EXERCISE — LOGICAL COMPARISONS

Choose the sentence that logically and correctly expresses the comparison.

1)   A. This year's standards are higher than last year.
       B. This year's standards are more high than last year.
       C. This year's standards are higher than last year's.

2)   A. Tom's attitudes are very different from his father's.
       B. Toms attitudes are very different from his father.
       C. Tom's attitudes are very different from his father.

3)   A. John is the stronger member of the gymnastics team.
       B. John is the strongest member of the gymnastics team.
       C. John is the most strong member of the gymnastics team.

4)   A. Tracy's book report was longer than Tony's.
       B. Tracy's book report was more long than Tony's.
       C. Tracy's book report was longer than Tony.

5)   A. Becoming a lawyer is as difficult as, if not more difficult than, becoming a doctor.

       B. Becoming a lawyer is as difficult, if not more difficult than, becoming a doctor.

       C. Becoming a lawyer is difficult, if not more difficult than, becoming a doctor.

6)   A. Better than any movie of the modern era, Schindler's List portrays the destructiveness of hate.

       B. More better than any movie of the modern era, Schindler's List portrays the destructiveness of hate.

       C. Better than any other movie of the modern era, Schindler's List portrays the destructiveness of hate.

ANSWER KEY: PRACTICE EXERCISE FOR LOGICAL COMPARISONS

1) C   Option C is correct because the comparison is between this year's standards and last year's [standards is understood]. Option A compares the standards to last year. In Option B, the faulty comparative *more high* should be higher.

2) A   Option A is incorrect because Tom's attitudes are compared to his father's [attitudes is understood]. Option B deletes the necessary apostrophe to show possession (Tom's), and the comparison is faulty with *attitudes* compared to father. While Option C uses the correct possessive, it retains the faulty comparison shown in Option B.

3) B   In Option B, John is correctly the strongest member of a team that consists of more than two people. Option A uses the comparative *stronger* (comparison of two items) rather than the superlative *stronges*t (comparison of more than two). Option C uses a faulty superlative *most strong*.

4) A   Option A is correct because the comparison is between Tracy's book report and Tony's (book report). Option B uses the faulty comparative *more long* instead of *longer*. Option C wrongly compares Tracy's book report to Tony.

5) A   In Option A, the dual comparison is correctly stated: *as difficult as*, *if not more difficult than*. Remember to test the dual comparison by taking out the intervening comparison. Option B deletes the necessary *as* after the first *difficult*. Option C deletes the *as* before and after the first *difficult*.

6) C   Option C includes the necessary word *other* in the comparison *better than any other movie*. The comparison in Option A is not complete, and Option B uses a faulty comparative *more better*.

Skill 14.4   Recognize standard punctuation and capitalization

Commas
Commas indicate a brief pause. They are used to set off dependent clauses and long introductory word groups, to separate words in a series, to set off unimportant material that interrupts the flow of the sentence, and to separate independent clauses joined by conjunctions.

Error:	After I finish my master's thesis I plan to work in Chicago.
Problem:	A comma is needed after an introductory dependent word group containing a subject and verb.
Correction:	*After I finish my master's thesis, I plan to work in Chicago.*
Error:	I washed waxed and vacuumed my car today.
Problem:	Nouns, phrases, or clauses in a list, as well as two or more coordinate adjectives that modify one word, should be separated by commas. Although the word *and* is sometimes considered optional, it is often necessary to clarify the meaning.
Correction:	*I washed, waxed, and vacuumed my car today.*
Error:	She was a talented dancer but she is mostly remembered for her singing ability.
Problem:	A comma is needed before a conjunction that joins two independent clauses (complete sentences).
Correction:	*She was a talented dancer, but she is mostly remembered for her singing ability.*
Error:	This incident is I think typical of what can happen when the community remains so divided.
Problem:	Commas are needed between nonessential words or words that interrupt the main clause.
Correction:	*This incident is, I think, typical of what can happen when the community remains so divided.*

Semicolons and colons

Semicolons are needed to separate two or more closely related independent clauses when the second clause is introduced by a transitional adverb. (These clauses may also be written as separate sentences, preferably by placing the adverb within the second sentence). **Colons** are used to introduce lists and to emphasize what follows.

Error: I climbed to the top of the mountain, it took me three hours.

Problem: A comma alone cannot separate two independent clauses. Instead, a semicolon is needed to separate two related sentences.

Correction: *I climbed to the top of the mountain; it took me three hours.*

Error: In the movie, asteroids destroyed Dallas, Texas, Kansas City, Missouri, and Boston, Massachusetts.

Problem: Semicolons are needed to separate items in a series that already contains internal punctuation.

Correction: *In the movie, asteroids destroyed Dallas, Texas; Kansas City, Missouri; and Boston, Massachusetts.*

Error: Essays will receive the following grades, A for excellent, B for good, C for average, and D for unsatisfactory.

Problem: A colon is needed to emphasize the information or list that follows.

Correction: *Essays will receive the following grades: A for excellent, B for good, C for average, and D for unsatisfactory.*

Error: The school carnival included: amusement rides, clowns, food booths, and a variety of games.

Problem: The material preceding the colon and the list that follows is not a complete sentence. Do not separate a verb (or preposition) from the object.

Correction: *The school carnival included amusement rides, clowns, food booths, and a variety of games.*

Apostrophes

Apostrophes are used to show either contractions or possession.

Error: She shouldnt be permitted to smoke cigarettes in the building.

Problem: An apostrophe is needed in a contraction in place of the missing letter.

Correction: *She shouldn't be permitted to smoke cigarettes in the building.*

Error: My cousins motorcycle was stolen from his driveway.

Problem: An apostrophe is needed to show possession.

Correction: *My cousin's motorcycle was stolen from his driveway.*
(Note: The use of the apostrophe before the letter "s" means that there is just one cousin. The plural form would read the following way: My cousins' motorcycle was stolen from their driveway.)

Error: The childrens new kindergarten teacher was also a singer.

Problem: An apostrophe is needed to show possession.

Correction: *The children's new kindergarten teacher was also a singer.*

Error: Children screams could be heard for miles.

Problem: An apostrophe and the letter "s" are needed in the sentence to show whose screams it is.

Correction: *Children's screams could be heard for miles.*
(Note: Because the word children is already plural, the apostrophe and s must be added afterward to show ownership.)

Quotation marks

In a quoted statement that is either declarative or imperative, place the period inside the closing quotation marks.

"The airplane crashed on the runway during takeoff."

If the quotation is followed by other words in the sentence, place a comma inside the closing quotation marks and a period at the end of the sentence.

> "The airplane crashed on the runway during takeoff," said the announcer.

In most instances in which a quoted title or expression occurs at the end of a sentence, the period is placed before either the single or double quotation marks.

> "The middle school readers were unprepared to understand Bryant's poem 'Thanatopsis.'"

> Early book-length adventure stories such as *Don Quixote* and *The Three Musketeers* were known as "picaresque novels."

The final quotation mark would precede the period if the content of the sentence were about a speech or quote because the understanding of the meaning would be confused by the placement of the period.

> The first thing out of his mouth was "Hi, I'm home."
> *but*
> The first line of his speech began "I arrived home to an empty house".

In sentences that are interrogatory or exclamatory, the question mark or exclamation point should be positioned outside the closing quotation marks if the quote itself is a statement or command or cited title.

> Who decided to lead us in the recitation of the "Pledge of Allegiance"?

> Why was Tillie shaking as she began her recitation, "Once upon a midnight dreary..."?

> I was embarrassed when Mrs. White said, "Your slip is showing"!

In sentences that are declarative but the quotation is a question or an exclamation, place the question mark or exclamation point inside the quotation marks.

> The hall monitor yelled, "Fire! Fire!"
> "Fire! Fire!" yelled the hall monitor.

> Cory shrieked, "Is there a mouse in the room?" (In this instance, the question supersedes the exclamation.)

Quotations—whether words, phrases, or clauses—should be punctuated according to the rules of the grammatical function they serve in the sentence.

The works of Shakespeare, "the bard of Avon," have been contested as originating with other authors.

"You'll get my money," the old man warned, "when 'hell freezes over'."

Sheila cited the passage that began "Four score and seven years ago...." (Note the ellipsis followed by an enclosed period.)

"Old Ironsides" inspired the preservation of the U.S.S. Constitution. Use quotation marks to enclose the titles of shorter works: songs, short poems, short stories, essays, and chapters of books. (See "Using Italics" for punctuating longer titles.)

"The Tell-Tale Heart"   "Casey at the Bat"   "America the Beautiful"

Dashes and Italics

Place **dashes** to denote sudden breaks in thought.

Some periods in literature—the Romantic Age, for example— spanned different periods in different countries.

Use dashes instead of commas for amplification or explanation if commas are already used elsewhere in the sentence.

The Fireside Poets included three Brahmans—James Russell Lowell, Henry David Wadsworth, Oliver Wendell Holmes—and John Greenleaf Whittier.

Use **italics** to punctuate the titles of long works of literature; names of periodical publications; musical scores; works of art; and motion picture, television, and radio programs. (When unable to write in italics, students should be instructed to underline in their own writing where italics would be appropriate.)

The Idylls of the King   *Hiawatha*   *The Sound and the Fury*
Mary Poppins   *Newsweek*   *The Nutcracker Suite*

Capitalize all proper names of persons (including specific organizations or agencies of government); places (countries, states, cities, parks, and specific geographical areas); things (political parties, structures, historical and cultural terms, and calendar and time designations); and religious terms (any deity, revered person or group, sacred writings).

Percy Bysshe Shelley, Argentina, Mount Rainier National Park, Grand Canyon, League of Nations, the Sears Tower, Birmingham, Lyric Theater, Americans, Midwesterners, Democrats, Renaissance, Boy Scouts of America, Easter, God, Bible, Dead Sea Scrolls, Koran

Capitalize proper adjectives and titles used with proper names.

California Gold Rush, President John Adams, French fries, Homeric epic, Romanesque architecture, Senator John Glenn

Note: Some words that represent titles and offices are not capitalized unless used with a proper name.

Capitalized	Not Capitalized
Congressman McKay	the congressman from Florida
Commander Alger	commander of the Pacific Fleet
Queen Elizabeth	the queen of England

Capitalize all main words in titles of works of literature, art, and music.

Error: Emma went to Dr. Peters for treatment since her own Doctor was on vacation.

Problem: The use of capital letters with *Emma* and *Dr .Peters* is correct since they are specific (proper) names; the title *Dr.* is also capitalized. However, the word *doctor* is not a specific name and should not be capitalized.

Correction: *Emma went to Dr. Peters for treatment since her own doctor was on vacation.*

Error: Our Winter Break does not start until next wednesday.

Problem: Days of the week are capitalized, but seasons are not capitalized.

Correction: *Our winter break does not start until next Wednesday.*

Error: The exchange student from israel who came to study biochemistry spoke spanish very well.

Problem: Languages and the names of countries are always capitalized. Courses are also capitalized when they refer to a specific course; they are not capitalized when they refer to courses in general.

Correction: *The exchange student from Israel who came to study Biochemistry spoke Spanish very well.*

PRACTICE EXERCISE – CAPITALIZATION AND PUNCTUATION

Choose the option that corrects an error in the underlined portion(s). If no error exists, choose "No change is necessary."

1) Greenpeace is an Organization that works to preserve the world's environment.

    A) greenpeace
    B) organization
    C) worlds
    D) No change is necessary

2) When our class travels to France next year, we will see the country's many famous landmarks.

    A) france
    B) year; we
    C) countries
    D) No change is necessary

3) New York City, the heaviest populated city in America has more than eight million people living there every day.

    A) new york city
    B) in America, has
    C) Every day
    D) No change is necessary

4) The television show The X-Files has gained a huge following because it focuses on paranormal phenomena, extraterrestrial life, and the oddities of human existence.

    A) Television
    B) following, because
    C) Human existence
    D) No change is necessary

5) Being a Policeman requires having many qualities: physical agility, good reflexes, and the ability to make quick decisions.

    A) policeman
    B) qualities;
    C) agility:
    D) No change is necessary

ANSWER KEY: PRACTICE EXERCISE FOR CAPITALIZATION AND PUNCTUATION

1. B   In the sentence, the word *organization* does not need to be capitalized due to the fact that it is a general noun. In Option A, the name of the organization should be capitalized. In Option C, the apostrophe is used to show that one world is being protected, not more than one.

2. D   In Option A, France is capitalized because it is the name of a country. In Option B, the comma, not the semi-colon, should separate a dependent clause from the main clause. In Option C, the use of an apostrophe and an "s" indicates only one country is being visited.

3. B   In Option A, *New York City* is capitalized because it is the name of a place. In Option B, a comma is needed to separate the noun *America*, from the verb *has*. In Option C, *every day* needs no capitalization.

4. D   In Option A, *television* does not need to be capitalized because it is a noun. In Option B, a comma is necessary to separate an independent clause from the main clause. In Option C, *human existence* is a general term that does not need capitalization.

5. A   In Option A, *policeman* does not need capitalization because it is a general noun. In Option B, a colon, not a semi-colon, is needed because the rest of the sentence is related to the main clause. In Option C, a comma, not a colon, is needed to separate the adjectives.

Sample Test: Writing

DIRECTIONS: *The passage below contains many errors. Read the passage. Then answer each test item by choosing the option that corrects an error in the underlined portion(s). No more than one underlined error will appear in each item. If no error exists, choose "No change is necessary."*

Climbing to the top of Mount Everest is an adventure. One which everyone—whether physically fit or not—seems eager to try. The trail stretches for miles, the cold temperatures are usually frigid and brutal.

Climbers must endure several barriers on the way including other hikers, steep jagged rocks, and lots of snow. Plus, climbers often find the most grueling part of the trip is their climb back down, just when they are feeling greatly exhausted. Climbers who take precautions are likely to find the ascent less arduous than the unprepared. By donning heavy flannel shirts, gloves, and hats, climbers prevented hypothermia, as well as simple frostbite. A pair of rugged boots is one of the necessities. If climbers are to avoid becoming dehydrated, there is beverages available for them to transport as well.

Once climbers are completely ready to begin their lengthy journey, they can comfortable enjoy the wonderful scenery. Wide rock formations dazzle the observers eyes with shades of gray and white, while the peak forms a triangle that seems to touch the sky. Each of the climbers are reminded of the splendor and magnifisence of Gods great Earth.

1. A pair of rugged boots is one of the necessities.
   (Rigorous) (Skill 12.2)

   A. are
   B. also one
   C. necesities
   D. No change is necessary

2. Climbing to the top of Mount Everest is an adventure. One which everyone—whether physically fit or not—seems eager to try.
   (Rigorous) (Skill 13.2)

   A. adventure, one
   B. people, whether
   C. seem
   D. No change is necessary

3. The trail stretches for miles, the cold temperatures are usually frigid and brutal.
   (Rigorous) (Skill 13.2)

   A. trails
   B. miles;
   C. usual
   D. No change is necessary

4. Climbers must endure <u>several</u> barriers <u>on the way including</u> other <u>hikers,</u> steep jagged rocks, and lots of snow.
(Average Rigor) (Skill 13.2)

A. severel
B. on the way, including
C. hikers'
D. No change is necessary

5. If climbers are to avoid <u>becoming</u> dehydrated, there <u>is</u> beverages available for <u>them</u> to transport as well.
(Easy) (Skill 13.3)

A. becomming
B. are
C. him
D. No change is necessary

6. Each of the climbers <u>are</u> reminded of the splendor and <u>magnifisence</u> of <u>God's</u> great Earth.
(Rigorous) (Skill 13.3)

A. is
B. magnifisence
C. Gods
D. No change is necessary

7. Plus, climbers often find the most grueling part of the trip is <u>their</u> climb back <u>down, just</u> when they <u>are</u> feeling greatly exhausted.
(Average Rigor) (Skill 14.1)

A. his
B. down; just
C. were
D. No change is necessary

8. By donning heavy flannel shirts, boots, and <u>hats, climbers</u> <u>prevented</u> hypothermia, as well as simple frostbite.
(Average Rigor) (Skill 14.1)

A. hats climbers
B. can prevent
C. hypothermia;
D. No change is necessary

9. Wide rock formations dazzle the <u>observers eyes</u> with shades of gray and <u>white, while</u> the peak <u>forms</u> a triangle that seems to touch the sky.
(Rigorous) (Skill 14.2)

A. observers' eyes
B. white; while
C. formed
D. No change is necessary

10. <u>Climbers who</u> take precautions are likely to find the ascent <u>less difficult</u> <u>then</u> the unprepared.
(Average Rigor) (Skill 14.3)

A. Climbers, who
B. least difficult
C. than
D. No change is necessary

11. Once climbers are completely prepared for <u>their</u> lengthy <u>journey, they</u> can <u>comfortable</u> enjoy the wonderful scenery.
(Easy) (Skill 14.3)

A. they're
B. journey; they
C. comfortably
D. No change is necessary

DIRECTIONS: *The passage below contains several errors. Read the passage. Then answer each test item by choosing the option that corrects an error in the underlined portion(s). No more than one underlined error will appear in each item. If no error exists, choose "No change is necessary."*

Every job places different kinds of demands on their employees. For example, whereas such jobs as accounting and bookkeeping require mathematical ability; graphic design requires creative/artistic ability.

Doing good at one job does not usually guarantee success at another. However, one of the elements crucial to all jobs are especially notable: the chance to accomplish a goal.

The accomplishment of the employees varies according to the job. In many jobs the employees become accustom to the accomplishment provided by the work they do every day.

In medicine, for example, every doctor tests him self by treating badly injured or critically ill people. In the operating room, a team of Surgeons, is responsible for operating on many of these patients. In addition to the feeling of accomplishment that the workers achieve, some jobs also give a sense of identity to the employees'. Professions such as law, education, and sales offer huge financial and emotional rewards. Politicians are public servants: who work for the federal and state governments. President bush is basically employed by the American people to make laws and run the country.

Finally; the contributions that employees make to their companies and to the world cannot be taken for granted. Through their work, employees are performing a service for their employers and are contributing something to the world.

12. <u>Professions</u> such as law, education, and sales <u>offer</u> huge <u>financial and</u> emotional rewards. (Rigorous) (Skill 13.2)

A. Profesions
B. financial, and
C. offered
D. No change is necessary

13. <u>For example, whereas</u> such jobs as accounting and bookkeeping require mathematical <u>ability;</u> graphic design requires creative/artistic ability. (Average Rigor) (Skill 13.2)

A. For example
B. whereas,
C. ability,
D. No change is necessary

14. <u>However,</u> one of the elements crucial to all jobs <u>are</u> especially <u>notable:</u> the accomplishment of a goal. (Average Rigor) (Skill 13.3)

A. However
B. is
C. notable;
D. No change is necessary

15. The <u>accomplishment</u> of the <u>employees</u> <u>varies</u> according to the job.
(Rigorous) (Skill 13.3)

A. accomplishment,
B. employee's
C. vary
D. No change is necessary

16. In many jobs the employees <u>become</u> <u>accustom</u> to the accomplishment <u>provided</u> by the work they do every day.
(Average Rigor) (Skill 14.1)

A. became
B. accustomed
C. provides
D. No change is necessary

17. Every job <u>places</u> different kinds of demands on <u>their</u> <u>employees</u>.
(Rigorous) (Skill 14.2)

A. place
B. its
C. employes
D. No change is necessary

18. In medicine, for example, every doctor <u>tests</u> <u>him self</u> by treating badly injured and critically ill people.
(Average Rigor) (Skill 14.2)

A. test
B. himself
C. critical
D. No change is necessary

19. In addition to the feeling of accomplishment that the workers <u>achieve</u>, some jobs also <u>give</u> a sense of self-identity to the <u>employees'</u>.
(Average Rigor) (Skill 14.2)

A. acheive
B. gave
C. employees
D. No change is necessary

20. Doing <u>good</u> at one job does not <u>usually</u> guarantee <u>success</u> at another.
(Rigorous) (Skill 14.3)

A. well
B. usualy
C. succeeding
D. No change is necessary

21. In the <u>operating room,</u> a team of <u>Surgeons, is</u> responsible for operating on many of <u>these</u> patients.
(Easy) (Skill 14.4)

A. operating room:
B. surgeons is
C. those
D. No change is necessary

22. Politicians <u>are</u> public <u>servants: who</u> <u>work</u> for the federal and state governments.
(Easy) (Skill 14.4)

A. were
B. servants who
C. worked
D. No change is necessary

23. **President bush is basically employed <u>by</u> the American people to <u>make</u> laws and run the country.**
(Easy) (Skill 14.4)

   A. Bush
   B. to
   C. made
   D. No change is necessary

24. **<u>Finally;</u> the contributions that employees make to <u>their</u> companies and to the world cannot be <u>taken</u> for granted.**
(Average Rigor) (Skill 14.4)

   A. Finally,
   B. their
   C. took
   D. No change is necessary

DIRECTIONS: *For the underlined sentence(s), choose the option that expresses the meaning with the most fluency and the clearest logic within the context. If the underlined sentence should not be changed, choose Option A, which shows no change.*

25. **Selecting members of a President's cabinet can often be an aggravating process. <u>Either there are too many or too few qualified candidates for a certain position, and then they have to be confirmed by the Senate, where there is the possibility of rejection.</u>**
(Rigorous) (Skill 12.3)

   A. Either there are too many or too few qualified candidate for a certain position, and then they have to be confirmed by the Senate, where there is the possibility of rejection.

   B. Qualified candidates for certain positions face the possibility of rejection, when they have to be confirmed by the Senate.

   C. The Senate has to confirm qualified candidates, who face the possibility of rejection.

   D. Because the Senate has to confirm qualified candidates; they face the possibility of rejection.

26. Treating patients for drug and/or alcohol abuse is a sometimes difficult process. Even though there are a number of different methods for helping the patient overcome a dependency, there is no way of knowing which is best in the long run.
(Rigorous) (Skill 12.3)

A. Even though there are a number of different methods for helping the patient overcome a dependency, there is no way of knowing which is best in the long run.

B. Even though different methods can help a patient overcome a dependency, there is no way to know which is best in the long run.

C. Even though there is no way to know which way is best in the long run, patients can overcome their dependencies when they are helped.

D. There is no way to know which method will help the patient overcome a dependency in the long run, even though there are many different ones.

27. Many factors account for the decline in quality of public education. Overcrowding, budget cutbacks, and societal deterioration which have greatly affected student learning.
(Rigorous) (Skill 12.3)

A. Overcrowding, budget cutbacks, and societal deterioration, which have greatly affected student learning.

B. Student learning has been greatly affected by overcrowding, budget cutbacks, and societal deterioration.

C. Due to overcrowding, budget cutbacks, and societal deterioration, student learning has been greatly affected.

D. Overcrowding, budget cutbacks, and societal deterioration have affected students learning greatly.

DIRECTIONS: *Choose the most effective word within the context of the sentence.*

28. **Many of the clubs in Boca Raton are noted for their _____ elegance.**
   (Average Rigor) (Skill 12.3)

   A. vulgar
   B. tasteful
   C. ordinary

29. **When a student is expelled from school, the parents are usually _____ in advance.**
   (Average Rigor) (Skill 12.3)

   A. rewarded
   B. congratulated
   C. notified

30. **Before appearing in court, the witness was _____ the papers requiring her to show up.**
   (Average Rigor) (Skill 12.3)

   A. condemned
   B. served
   C. criticized

DIRECTIONS: *Choose the underlined word or phrase that is unnecessary within the context of the passage.*

31. **Considered by many to be one of the worst terrorist incidents on American soil was the bombing of the Oklahoma City Federal Building which will be remembered for years to come.**
   (Average Rigor) (Skill 13.1)

   A. considered by many to be
   B. terrorist
   C. on American soil
   D. for years to come

32. **The flu epidemic struck most of the respected faculty and students of the Woolbright School , forcing the Boynton Beach School superintendent to close it down for two weeks.**
   (Average Rigor) (Skill 13.1)

   A. flu
   B. most of
   C. respected
   D. for two weeks

33. The <u>expanding</u> number of television channels has <u>prompted</u> cable operators to raise their prices, <u>even though</u> many consumers do not want to pay a higher <u>increased</u> amount for their service.
(Easy) (Skill 13.1)

A. expanding
B. prompted
C. even though
D. increased

DIRECTIONS: *Choose the sentence that logically and correctly expresses the comparison.*

(Easy) (Skill 14.3)

34. A. The Empire State Building in New York is taller than buildings in the city.

B. The Empire State Building in New York is taller than any other building in the city.

C. The Empire State Building in New York is tallest than other buildings in the city.

DIRECTIONS: *The passage below contains several errors. Read the passage. Then answer each test item by choosing the option that corrects an error in the underlined portion(s). No more than one underlined error will appear in each item. If no error exists, choose "No change is necessary."*

The discovery of a body at Paris Point marina in Boca Raton shocked the residents of Palmetto Pines, a luxury condominium complex located next door to the marina.

The victim is a thirty-five-year-old woman who had been apparently bludgeoned to death and dumped in the ocean late last night. Many neighbors reported terrible screams and gunshots: as well as the sound of a car backfiring loudly to Boca Raton Police shortly after midnight. The woman had been spotted in the lobby of Palmetto Pines around ten thirty, along with an older man, estimated to be in his fifties, and a younger man, in his late twenties.

"Apparently, the victim had been driven to the complex by the older man and was seen arguing with him when the younger man intervened", said Sheriff Fred Adams, "all three of them left the building together and walked to the marina, where gunshots rang out an hour later." Deputies found five bullets on the sidewalk and some blood, along with a steel pipe that is assumed to be the murder weapon. Two men were seen fleeing the scene in a red Mercedes short after, rushing toward the Interstate.

The Palm Beach County Coroner, Melvin Watts, said he concluded the victim's skull had been crushed by a blunt tool, which resulted in a brain hemorrhage. As of now, there is no clear motive for the murder.

35. **The victim <u>is</u> a thirty-five-year- old who had been apparently <u>bludgeoned</u> to death and dumped in the <u>ocean late</u> last night. (Rigorous) (Skill 14.1)**

    A. was
    B. bludgoned
    C. ocean: late
    D. No change is necessary

36. **Deputies found five bullets on the sidewalk and some <u>blood,</u> along with a steel pipe that is <u>assumed to be</u> the murder weapon. (Rigorous) (Skill 14.1)**

    A. blood;
    B. assuming
    C. to have been
    D. No change is necessary

37. **Two men <u>were</u> seen fleeing the scene in a red Mercedes <u>short</u> after, <u>rushing</u> toward the Interstate. (Easy) (Skill 14.3)**

    A. are
    B. shortly
    C. rushed
    D. No change is necessary

38. The discovery of a body at Paris Point <u>marina</u> in Boca Raton shocked the <u>residents</u> of Palmetto Pines, a luxury <u>condominium</u> complex located next door to the marina.
(Easy) (Skill 14.4)

A. Marina
B. residence
C. condominium
D. No change is necessary

39. Many <u>neighbors</u> reported terrible screams and <u>gunshots: as</u> well as the sound of a car backfiring <u>loudly</u> to Boca Raton Police shortly after midnight.
(Average Rigor) (Skill 14.4)

A. neighbors
B. gunshots, as
C. loud
D. No change is necessary

40. The woman <u>had</u> been spotted in the lobby of Palmetto Pines around ten <u>thirty,</u> along with an older <u>man, estimated</u> to be in his fifties, and a younger man in his late twenties.
(Rigorous) (Skill 14.4)

A. has
B. thirty;
C. man estimated
D. No change is necessary

41. "Apparently, the victim had been driven to the complex by the older man, and was seen arguing with him when the younger man intervened," said <u>Sheriff Fred Adams, "all</u> three of them left the building together and walked to the marina, when gunshots rang out an hour later."
(Average Rigor) (Skill 14.4)

A. sheriff Fred Adams, "all
B. sheriff Fred Adams, "All
C. Sheriff Fred Adams." All
D. No change is necessary

42. The Palm Beach County <u>Coroner, Melvin Watts,</u> said he concluded the victim's skull had been crushed by a blunt <u>tool that</u> resulted in a brain <u>hemorrhage</u>.
(Rigorous) (Skill 14.4)

A. tool, which
B. Coroner Melvin Watts,
C. hemorrage
D. No change is necessary

Answer Key — Writing

1.	B		22.	B
2.	A		23.	A
3.	B		24.	A
4.	B		25.	C
5.	B		26.	B
6.	A		27.	B
7.	D		28.	B
8.	B		29.	C
9.	A		30.	B
10.	C		31.	A
11.	C		32.	C
12.	D		33.	D
13.	C		34.	B
14.	B		35.	A
15.	C		36.	C
16.	B		37.	B
17.	B		38.	A
18.	B		39.	B
19.	C		40.	C
20.	A		41.	C
21.	B		42.	A

Rigor Table: Writing

	Easy 20%	Average 40%	Rigorous 40%
Questions (42)	5, 11, 21, 22, 23, 33, 34, 37, 38	4, 7, 8, 10, 13, 14, 16, 18, 19, 24, 28, 29, 30, 31, 32, 39, 41	1, 2, 3, 6, 9, 12, 15, 17, 20, 25, 26, 27, 35, 36, 40, 42
TOTALS	9 (21%)	17 (40.5%)	16 (38.1%)

Rationales with Sample Questions: Writing

1. **A pair of rugged boots <u>is one</u> of the <u>necessities</u>.**
   (Rigorous) (Skill 12.2)

   A. are
   B. also one
   C. necesities
   D. No change is necessary

Answer: B. also one

Option B is correct because the transition *also* is needed to continue the list of necessary items from the previous sentence. Option A is incorrect because the singular verb *is* must agree with the singular noun *pair* (a collective singular). Option C is incorrect because *necessities* is spelled correctly in the text.

2. **Climbing to the top of Mount Everest is an <u>adventure. One</u> which everyone—<u>whether</u> physically fit or not—<u>seems</u> eager to try.**
   (Rigorous) (Skill 13.2)

   A. adventure, one
   B. people, whether
   C. seem
   D. No change is necessary

Answer: A. adventure, one

A comma is needed between *adventure* and *one* to avoid creating a fragment of the second part. In Option B, a comma after *everyone* would not be appropriate when the dash is used on the other side of *not*. In Option C, the singular verb *seems* is needed to agree with the singular subject *everyone*.

3. The <u>trail</u> stretches for <u>miles,</u>
the cold temperatures are
<u>usually</u> frigid and brutal.
(Rigorous) (Skill 13.2)

  A. trails
  B. miles;
  C. usual
  D. No change is necessary

Answer: B. miles

A semicolon, not a comma, is needed to separate the first independent clause from the second independent clause. Option A is incorrect because the plural subject *trails* needs the singular verb *stretch*. Option C is incorrect because the adverb form *usually* is needed to modify the adjective *frigid.*

4. Climbers must endure <u>several</u> barriers <u>on the way including</u> other
<u>hikers</u>, steep jagged rocks, and lots of snow.
(Average Rigor) (Skill 13.2)

  A. severel
  B. on the way, including
  C. hikers'
  D. No change is necessary

Answer: B. on the way, including

A comma is needed to set off the modifying phrase. Option A is incorrect because the word *several* is already correct in the sentence. Option C is incorrect because no apostrophe is needed after *hikers* since possession is not involved.

5. If climbers are to avoid <u>becoming</u> dehydrated, there <u>is</u> beverages
available for them to transport as well.
(Easy) (Skill 13.3)

  A. becomming
  B. are
  C. him
  D. No change is necessary

Answer: B. are

The plural verb *are* must be used with the plural subject *beverages.* Option A is incorrect because *becoming* has only one "m." Option C is incorrect because the plural pronoun *them* is needed to agree with the referent *climbers.*

6.   Each of the climbers <u>are</u> reminded of the splendor and <u>magnifisence</u> of <u>God's</u> great Earth.
       (Rigorous) (Skill 13.3)

       A. is
       B. magnifisence
       C. Gods
       D. No change is necessary

Answer: A. is

The singular verb *is* agrees with the singular subject *each.* Option B is incorrect because *magnificence* is misspelled. Option C is incorrect because an apostrophe is needed to show possession.

7.   Plus, climbers often find the most grueling part of the trip is <u>their</u> climb back <u>down, just</u> when they <u>are</u> feeling greatly exhausted.
       (Average Rigor) (Skill 14.1)

       A. his
       B. down; just
       C. were
       D. No change is necessary

Answer: D. No change is necessary

The present tense must be used consistently throughout; therefore, Option C is incorrect. Option A is incorrect because the singular pronoun *his* does not agree with the plural antecedent *climbers.* Option B is incorrect because a comma, not a semicolon, is needed to separate the dependent clause from the main clause.

8.   By donning heavy flannel shirts, boots, and <u>hats, climbers</u> <u>prevented</u> hypothermia, as well as simple frostbite.
       (Average Rigor) (Skill 14.1)

       A. hats climbers
       B. can prevent
       C. hypothermia;
       D. No change is necessary

Answer: B. can prevent

The verb *prevented* is in the past tense and must be changed to the present *can prevent* to be consistent. Option A is incorrect because a comma is needed after a long introductory phrase. Option C is incorrect because the semicolon creates a fragment of the phrase *as well as simple frostbite.*

9.	Wide rock formations dazzle the <u>observers eyes</u> with shades of gray and <u>white, while</u> the peak <u>forms</u> a triangle that seems to touch the sky.
(Rigorous) (Skill 14.2)

A.	observers' eyes
B.	white; while
C.	formed
D.	No change is necessary

Answer: A. observers' eyes

An apostrophe is needed to show the plural possessive form *observers' eyes*. Option B is incorrect because the semicolon would make the second half of the item seem like an independent clause when the subordinating conjunction *while* makes that clause dependent. Option C is incorrect because *formed* is in the wrong tense.

10.	<u>Climbers who</u> take precautions are likely to find the ascent <u>less difficult</u> <u>then</u> the unprepared.
(Average Rigor) (Skill 14.3)

A.	Climbers, who
B.	least difficult
C.	than
D.	No change is necessary

Answer: C. than

Option C is correct because the comparative adverb *than*, not *then*, is needed. Option A is incorrect because a comma would make the phrase *who take precautions* seem less restrictive or less essential to the sentence. Option B is incorrect because *less* is appropriate when two items—the prepared and the unprepared—are compared.

11. Once climbers are completely prepared for <u>their</u> lengthy <u>journey,</u> <u>they</u> can <u>comfortable</u> enjoy the wonderful scenery.
(Easy) (Skill 14.3)

   A. they're
   B. journey; they
   C. comfortably
   D. No change is necessary

Answer: C. comfortably

The adverb form *comfortably* is needed to modify the verb phrase *can enjoy*. Option A is incorrect because the possessive plural pronoun is spelled *their*. Option B is incorrect because a semi-colon would make the first half of the item seem like an independent clause when the subordinating conjunction *once* makes that clause dependent.

12. <u>Professions</u> such as law, education, and sales <u>offer</u> huge <u>financial</u> <u>and</u> emotional rewards.
(Rigorous) (Skill 13.2)

   A. Profesions
   B. financial, and
   C. offered
   D. No change is necessary

Answer: D. No change is necessary.

Option A is incorrect because *professions* is spelled correctly in the sentence. Option B is incorrect because a comma is not needed to join compound objects of prepositions. In Option C, *offered*, is in the wrong tense.

13. <u>For example,</u> <u>whereas</u> such jobs as accounting and bookkeeping require mathematical <u>ability;</u> graphic design requires creative/artistic ability.
    (Average Rigor) (Skill 13.2)

    A. For example
    B. whereas,
    C. ability,
    D. No change is necessary

Answer: C. ability,

An introductory dependent clause is set off with a comma, not a semicolon. Option A is incorrect because the transitional phrase *for example* should be set off with a comma. Option B is incorrect because the adverb *whereas* functions as *while* and does not take a comma after it.

14. <u>However,</u> one of the elements crucial to all jobs <u>are</u> especially <u>notable:</u> the accomplishment of a goal.
    (Average Rigor) (Skill 13.3)

    A. However
    B. is
    C. notable;
    D. No change is necessary

Answer: B. is

The singular verb *is* is needed to agree with the singular subject *one.* Option A is incorrect because a comma is needed to set off the transitional word *however.* Option C is incorrect because a colon, not a semicolon, is needed to set off an item.

15. The <u>accomplishment</u> of the <u>employees</u> <u>varies</u> according to the job. (Rigorous) (Skill 13.3)

    A. accomplishment,
    B. employee's
    C. vary
    D. No change is necessary

Answer: C. vary

The singular verb *vary* is needed to agree with the singular subject *accomplishment*. Option A is incorrect because a comma after *accomplishment* would suggest that the modifying phrase *of the employees* is additional instead of essential. Option B is incorrect because *employees* is not possessive.

16. In many jobs, the employees <u>become</u> <u>accustom</u> to the accomplishment <u>provided</u> by the work they do every day. (Average Rigor) (Skill 14.1)

    A. became
    B. accustomed
    C. provides
    D. No change is necessary

Answer: B. accustomed

The past participle *accustomed* is needed with the verb *become*. Option A is incorrect because the verb tense does not need to change to the past *became*. Option C is incorrect because *provides* is the wrong tense.

17. Every job <u>places</u> different kinds of demands on <u>their</u> <u>employees</u>. (Rigorous) (Skill 14.2)

    A. place
    B. its
    C. employes
    D. No change is necessary

Answer: B. accustomed

The singular possessive pronoun *its* must agree with its antecedent *job*, which is singular also. Option A is incorrect because *place* is a plural form and the subject, *job*, is singular. Option C is incorrect because the correct spelling of *employees* is given in the sentence.

18. In medicine, for example, every doctor <u>tests</u> <u>him self</u> by treating badly injured and critically ill people.
(Average Rigor) (Skill 14.2)

   A. test
   B. himself
   C. critical
   D. No change is necessary

Answer: B. himself

The reflexive pronoun *himself* is needed. (Him self is nonstandard and never correct.) Option A is incorrect because the singular verb test is needed to agree with the singular subject *doctor*. Option C is incorrect because the adverb *critically* is needed to modify the verb *ill*.

19. In addition to the feeling of accomplishment that the workers <u>achieve</u>, some jobs also <u>give</u> a sense of self-identity to the <u>employees'</u>.
(Average Rigor) (Skill 14.2)

   A. acheive
   B. gave
   C. employees
   D. No change is necessary

Answer: C. employees

Option C is correct because *employees* is not possessive. Option A is incorrect because *achieve* is spelled correctly in the sentence. Option B is incorrect because *gave* is the wrong tense.

20. Doing <u>good</u> at one job does not <u>usually</u> guarantee <u>success</u> at another.
(Rigorous) (Skill 14.3)

   A. well
   B. usualy
   C. succeeding
   D. No change is necessary

Answer: A. well

The adverb *well* modifies the word *doing*. Option B is incorrect because *usually* is spelled correctly in the sentence. Option C is incorrect because *succeeding* is in the wrong tense.

21. In the <u>operating room,</u> a team of <u>Surgeons, is</u> responsible for operating on many of <u>these</u> patients.
   (Easy) (Skill 14.4)

   A. operating room:
   B. surgeons is
   C. those
   D. No change is necessary

Answer: B. surgeons is

Surgeons is not a proper name so it does not need to be capitalized. A comma is not needed to break up a team of surgeons from the rest of the sentence. Option A is incorrect because a comma, not a colon, is needed to set off an item. Option C is incorrect because *those* is an incorrect pronoun.

22. Politicians <u>are</u> public <u>servants: who</u> <u>work</u> for the federal and state governments.
   (Easy) (Skill 14.4)

   A. were
   B. servants who
   C. worked
   D. No change is necessary

Answer: B. servants who

A colon is not needed to set off the introduction of the sentence. In Option A, *were*, is the incorrect tense of the verb. In Option C, *worked*, is in the wrong tense.

23. President bush is basically employed <u>by</u> the American people to <u>make</u> laws and run the country.
   (Easy) (Skill 14.4)

   A. Bush
   B. to
   C. made
   D. No change is necessary

Answer: A. Bush

Bush is a proper name and it should be capitalized. Option B, *to*, does not fit with the verb *employed*. Option C uses the wrong form of the verb, *make*.

24. <u>Finally;</u> the contributions that employees make to <u>their</u> companies and to the world cannot be <u>taken</u> for granted.
(Average Rigor) (Skill 14.4)

    A. Finally,
    B. their
    C. took
    D. No change is necessary

Answer: A. Finally,

A comma is needed to separate *Finally* from the rest of the sentence. Finally is a preposition that usually heads a dependent sentence, hence, a comma is needed. Option B is incorrect because *their* is misspelled. Option C is incorrect because *took* is the wrong form of the verb.

25. Selecting members of a President's cabinet can often be an aggravating process. <u>Either there are too many or too few qualified candidates for a certain position, and then they have to be confirmed by the Senate, where there is the possibility of rejection.</u>
(Rigorous) (Skill 12.3)

    A. Either there are too many or too few qualified candidate for a certain position, and then they have to be confirmed by the Senate, where there is the possibility of rejection.

    B. Qualified candidates for certain positions face the possibility of rejection, when they have to be confirmed by the Senate.

    C. The Senate has to confirm qualified candidates, who face the possibility of rejection.

    D. Because the Senate has to confirm qualified candidates; they face the possibility of rejection.

Answer: C. The Senate has to confirm qualified candidates, who face the possibility of rejection.

Option C is the most straightforward and concise sentence. Option A is too unwieldy with the wordy *Either...or* phrase at the beginning. Option B does not make clear the fact that candidates face rejection by the Senate. Option D illogically implies that candidates face rejection because they have to be confirmed by the Senate.

26. **Treating patients for drug and/or alcohol abuse is a sometimes difficult process. <u>Even though there are a number of different methods for helping the patient overcome a dependency, there is no way of knowing which is best in the long-run.</u>
(Rigorous) (Skill 12.3)**

   A. Even though there are a number of different methods for helping the patient overcome a dependency, there is no way of knowing which is best in the long-run.

   B. Even though different methods can help a patient overcome a dependency, there is no way to know which is best in the long-run.

   C. Even though there is no way to know which way is best in the long run, patients can overcome their dependencies when they are helped.

   D. There is no way to know which method will help the patient overcome a dependency in the long run, even though there are many different ones.

Answer: B. Even though different methods can help a patient overcome a dependency, there is no way to know which is best in the long-run.

Option B is concise and logical. Option A tends to ramble with the use of *there are* and the verbs *helping* and *knowing*. Option C is awkwardly worded and repetitive in the first part of the sentence and vague in the second because it never indicates how the patients can be helped. Option D contains the unnecessary phrase *even though there are many different ones.*

27. **Many factors account for the decline in quality of public education. <u>Overcrowding, budget cutbacks, and societal deterioration which have greatly affected student learning.</u>**
(Rigorous) (Skill 12.3)

    A. Overcrowding, budget cutbacks, and societal deterioration which have greatly affected student learning.

    B. Student learning has been greatly affected by overcrowding, budget cutbacks, and societal deterioration.

    C. Due to overcrowding, budget cutbacks, and societal deterioration, student learning has been greatly affected.

    D. Overcrowding, budget cutbacks, and societal deterioration have affected students learning greatly.

Answer: B. Student learning has been greatly affected by overcrowding, budget cutbacks, and societal deterioration.

Option B is concise and best explains the causes of the decline in student education. The unnecessary use of *which* in Option A makes the sentence feel incomplete. Option C has weak coordination between the reasons for the decline in public education and the fact that student learning has been affected. Option D incorrectly places the adverb *greatly* after learning, instead of before *affected.*

28. **Many of the clubs in Boca Raton are noted for their _____ elegance.**
(Average Rigor) (Skill 12.3)

    A. vulgar
    B. tasteful
    C. ordinary

Answer: B. tasteful

Tasteful means beautiful or charming, which would correspond to an elegant club. The words *vulgar* and *ordinary* have negative connotations.

29. **When a student is expelled from school, the parents are usually _____ in advance.**
(Average Rigor) (Skill 12.3)

    A. rewarded
    B. congratulated
    C. notified

Answer: C. notified

Notified means "informed or told," which fits into the logic of the sentence. The words *rewarded* and *congratulated* are positive actions, which do not make sense regarding someone being expelled from school.

30. **Before appearing in court, the witness was _____ the papers requiring her to show up.**
(Average Rigor) (Skill 12.3)

    A. condemned
    B. served
    C. criticized

Answer: B. served

Served means "given," which makes sense in the context of the sentence. *Condemned* and *criticized* do not make sense within the context of the sentence.

31. **Considered by many to be one of the worst terrorist incidents on American soil was the bombing of the Oklahoma City Federal Building which will be remembered for years to come.**
(Average Rigor) (Skill 13.1)

    A. considered by many to be
    B. terrorist
    C. on American soil
    D. for years to come

Answer: A. considered by many to be

Considered by many to be is a wordy phrase and unnecessary in the context of the sentence. All other words are necessary within the context of the sentence.

32. The <u>flu</u> epidemic struck <u>most of</u> the <u>respected</u> faculty and students of the Woolbright School, forcing the Boynton Beach School Superintendent to close it down <u>for two weeks.</u>
(Average Rigor) (Skill 13.1)

    A. flu
    B. most of
    C. respected
    D. for two weeks

Answer: C. respected

The fact that the faculty might have been *respected* is not necessary to mention in the sentence. The other words and phrases are all necessary to complete the meaning of the sentence.

33. The <u>expanding</u> number of television channels has <u>prompted</u> cable operators to raise their prices, <u>even though</u> many consumers do not want to pay a higher <u>increased</u> amount for their service.
(Easy) (Skill 13.1)

    A. expanding
    B. prompted
    C. even though
    D. increased

Answer: D. increased

The word *increased* is redundant with higher and should be removed. All the other words are necessary within the context of the sentence.

34. **Choose the sentence that logically and correctly expresses the comparison.**
(Easy) (Skill 14.3)

   A. The Empire State Building in New York is taller than buildings in the city.

   B. The Empire State Building in New York is taller than any other building in the city.

   C. The Empire State Building in New York is tallest than other buildings in the city.

Answer: B. The Empire State Building in New York is taller than any other building in the city.

Because the Empire State Building is a building in New York City, the phrase *any other* must be included. Option A is incorrect because the Empire State Building is implicitly compared to itself since it is one of the buildings. Option C is incorrect because *tallest i*s the incorrect form of the adjective.

35. **The victim is a thirty-five-year-old who had been apparently bludgeoned to death and dumped in the ocean late last night.**
(Rigorous) (Skill 14.1)

   A. was
   B. bludgeoned
   C. ocean: late
   D. No change is necessary

Answer: A. was

The past tense *was* is needed to maintain consistency. Option B creates a misspelling. Option C incorrectly uses a colon when none is needed.

36. Deputies found five bullets on the sidewalk and some <u>blood,</u> along with a steel pipe that is <u>assumed</u> <u>to be</u> the murder weapon.
(Rigorous) (Skill 14.1)

A. blood;
B. assuming
C. to have been
D. No change is necessary

Answer: C. to have been

The past tense *to have been* is needed to maintain consistency. Option A incorrectly uses a colon, instead of a comma. Option B uses the wrong form of the verb *assumed.*

37. Two men <u>were</u> seen fleeing the scene in a red Mercedes <u>short</u> after, <u>rushing</u> toward the Interstate.
(Easy) (Skill 14.3)

A. are
B. shortly
C. rushed
D. No change is necessary

Answer: B. shortly

The adverb *shortly* is needed instead of the adjective short. Option A incorrectly uses the present tense *are* instead of the past tense *were.* Option C, *rushed,* is the wrong form of the verb.

38. The discovery of a body at Paris Point <u>marina</u> in Boca Raton shocked the <u>residents</u> of Palmetto Pines, a luxury <u>condominium</u> complex located next door to the marina.
(Easy) (Skill 14.4)

A. Marina
B. residence
C. condominium
D. No change is necessary

Answer: A. Marina

Marina is a name that needs to be capitalized. Options B and C create misspellings.

39. Many <u>neighbors</u> reported terrible screams and <u>gunshots: as</u> well as the sound of a car backfiring <u>loudly</u> to Boca Raton Police shortly after midnight.
(Average Rigor) (Skill 14.4)

    A. neighbors
    B. gunshots, as
    C. loud
    D. No change is necessary

Answer: B. gunshots, as

Option B correctly uses a comma, not a colon, to separate the items. Option A creates a misspelling. Option C incorrectly changes the adverb into an adjective.

40. The woman <u>had</u> been spotted in the lobby of Palmetto Pines around ten <u>thirty,</u> along with an older <u>man, estimated</u> to be in his fifties, and a younger man in his late twenties.
(Rigorous) (Skill 14.4)

    A. has
    B. thirty;
    C. man estimated
    D. No change is necessary

Answer: C. man estimated

A comma is not needed to separate the item because an older man estimated to be in his fifties is one complete fragment. Option A incorrectly uses the present tense *has* instead of the past tense *had*. Option B incorrectly uses a colon when a comma is needed.

41. "Apparently, the victim had been driven to the complex by the older man, and was seen arguing with him when the younger man intervened," said <u>Sheriff Fred Adams, "all</u> three of them left the building together and walked to the marina, when gunshots rang out an hour later."
(Average Rigor) (Skill 14.4)

A. sheriff Fred Adams, "all
B. sheriff Fred Adams, "All
C. Sheriff Fred Adams." All
D. No change is necessary

Answer: C. Sheriff Fred Adams." All

The quote's source comes in the middle of two independent clauses, so a period should follow *Adams*. Option A is incorrect because titles, when they come before a name, must be capitalized. Punctuation is also faulty. Option B is incorrect because the word *Adams* ends a sentence; a comma is not strong enough to support two sentences.

42. The Palm Beach County <u>Coroner, Melvin Watts,</u> said he concluded the victim's skull had been crushed by a blunt <u>tool that</u> resulted in a brain <u>hemorrhage</u>.
(Rigorous) (Skill 14.4)

A. tool, which
B. Coroner Melvin Watts,
C. hemorrhage
D. No change is necessary

Answer: A. tool, which

Option A is correct because the use of *which* refers to things other than humans and is used to introduce nonessential clauses. Option B is incorrect because the commas are needed between nonessential phrases or words that interrupt the main clause. Option C offers a misspelling of *hemorrhage*.

COMPETENCY 15.0 DEMONSTRATE THE ABILITY TO PREPARE A DEVELOPED COMPOSITION ON A GIVEN TOPIC USING LANGUAGE AND STYLE APPROPRIATE TO A GIVE AUDIENCE, PURPOSE, AND OCCASION

On the Basic Skills exam, you will be required to write a constructed response essay in which you are expected to:

- Compose a coherent, focused, and sustained composition on a given topic using language and style appropriate to a specified audience, purpose, and occasion
- State and maintain a clear thesis statement using organizational strategies to enhance meaning and clarity
- Provide reasoned support and/or specific examples to maintain the thesis statement
- Use effective sentence structure, word choice, and mechanics (e.g. grammar, syntax)
- Use spelling, capitalization, and punctuation according to the conventions of Standard American English.

Your response will be evaluated based on the following criteria:

• **Appropriateness:** the extent to which the response addresses the topic and uses language and style appropriate for the specified audience, purpose, and occasion

• **Focus and Organization:** the extent to which the response states and maintains the thesis statement by using organizational strategies to enhance meaning and clarity

• **Support:** the extent to which the response provides reasoned support and specific examples to develop the thesis

• **Grammar, Sentence Structure, and Usage:** the extent to which the response uses appropriate grammar, effective sentence structure, and precise usage

• **Conventions:** the extent to which the response demonstrates the ability to spell common words and to use the conventions of capitalization and punctuation accurately

Your response will be evaluated based on your demonstrated ability to express and support opinions, not on the nature or content of the opinions expressed. The final version of your response should conform to the conventions of Standard American English. Your response should be your original work, written in your own words, and not copied or paraphrased from some other work.

ESSAY GUIDELINES

Even before you select a topic, determine what each prompt is asking you to discuss. This first decision is crucial. If you pick a topic you do not really understand or about which you have little to say, you will have difficulty developing your essay. So take a few moments to analyze each topic carefully *before* you begin to write.

Topic A: A modern invention that can be considered a wonder of the world

In general, the topic prompts have two parts:
the *SUBJECT* of the topic and
an *ASSERTION* about the subject.

The **subject** is *a modern invention*. In this prompt, the word *modern* indicates you should discuss something invented recently, at least in this century. The word *invention* indicates you are to write about something created by humans (not natural phenomena such as mountains or volcanoes). You may discuss an invention that has potential for harm, such as chemical warfare or the atomic bomb, or you may discuss an invention that has the potential for good: the computer, DNA testing, television, antibiotics, and so on.

The **assertion** (a statement of point of view) is that *the invention has such powerful or amazing qualities that it should be considered a wonder of the world*. The assertion states your point of view about the subject, and it limits the range for discussion. In other words, you would discuss particular qualities or uses of the invention, not just discuss how it was invented or whether it should have been invented at all.

Note also that this particular topic encourages you to use examples to show the reader that a particular invention is a modern wonder. Some topic prompts lend themselves to essays with an argumentative edge, one in which you take a stand on a particular issue and persuasively prove your point. Here, you undoubtedly could offer examples or illustrations of the many *wonders* and uses of the particular invention you chose.

Be aware that misreading or misinterpreting the topic prompt can lead to serious problems. Papers that do not address the topic occur when one reads too quickly or only half understands the topic. This may happen if you misread or misinterpret words. Misreading can also lead to a paper that addresses only part of the topic prompt rather than the entire topic.

To develop a complete essay, spend a few minutes planning. Jot down your ideas and quickly sketch an outline. Although you may feel under pressure to begin writing, you will write more effectively if you plan your major points.

Prewriting

Before actually writing, you will need to generate content and to develop a writing plan. Three prewriting techniques that can be helpful are:

Brainstorming

When brainstorming, quickly create a list of words and ideas that are connected to the topic. Let your mind roam free to generate as many relevant ideas as possible in a few minutes. For example, on the topic of computers you may write

> Computer — modern invention
> Types — personal computers, microchips in calculators and watches
> Wonder — acts like an electronic brain
> Uses — science, medicine, offices, homes, schools
> Problems — too much reliance; the machines are not perfect

This list could help you focus on the topic and states the points you could develop in the body paragraphs. The brainstorming list keeps you on track and is well worth the few minutes it takes to jot down the ideas. While you have not ordered the ideas, seeing them on paper is an important step.

Questioning

Questioning helps you focus as you mentally ask a series of exploratory questions about the topic. You may use the most basic questions: **who, what, where, when, why, and how.**

"**What** is my subject?"
> [computers]

"**What** types of computers are there?"
> [personal computers, microchip computers]

"**Why** have computers been a positive invention?"
> [act like an electronic brain in machinery and equipment; help solve complex scientific problems]

"**How** have computers been a positive invention?"
> [used to make improvements in
> - science (space exploration, moon landings)
> - medicine (MRIs, CT scans, surgical tools, research models)
> - business (PCs, FAX, telephone equipment)
> - education (computer programs for math, languages, science, social studies)
> - personal use (family budgets, tax programs, healthy diet plans)]

"How can I show that computers are good?"
    [citing numerous examples]

"What problems do I see with computers?"
    [too much reliance, not yet perfect.]

"What personal experiences would help me develop examples to respond to this topic?
    [my own experiences using computers]

Of course, you may not have time to write out the questions completely. You might just write the words *who, what, where, why,* and *how* and the major points next to each. An abbreviated list might look as follows:

What — computers/modern wonder/making life better
How — through technological improvements: lasers, calculators, CT scans, MRIs.
Where — in science and space exploration, medicine, schools, offices

In a few moments, your questions should help you to focus on the topic and to generate interesting ideas and points to make in the essay. Later in the writing process, you can look back at the list to be sure you have made the key points you intended.

Clustering

Some visual thinkers find clustering an effective prewriting method. When clustering, you draw a box in the center of your paper and write your topic within that box. Then you draw lines from the center box and connect it to small satellite boxes that contain related ideas. Note the cluster below on computers:

SAMPLE CLUSTER

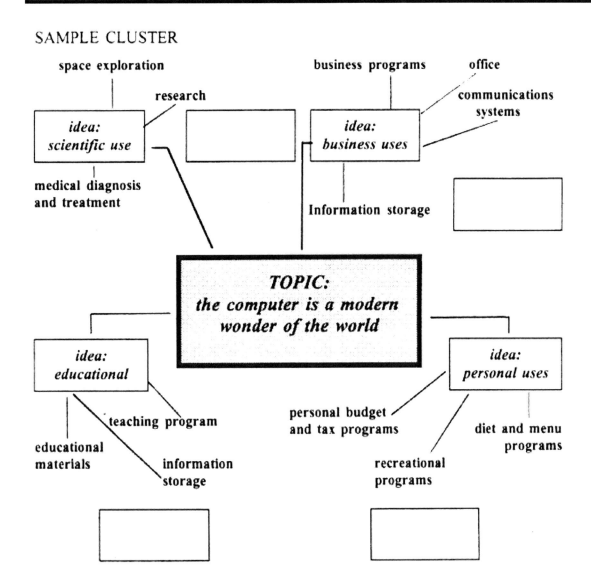

Writing the Thesis

After focusing on the topic and generating your ideas, form your thesis, the controlling idea of your essay. The thesis is your general statement to the reader that expresses your point of view and guides your essay's purpose and scope. The thesis should allow you either to explain your subject or to take an arguable position about it. A strong thesis statement is neither too narrow nor too broad.

Subject and Assertion of the Thesis

From the analysis of the general topic, you saw the topic in terms of its two parts—*subject* and *assertion*. On the exam, your thesis or viewpoint on a particular topic is stated in two important points:

1.   the *SUBJECT* of the paper

2.   the *ASSERTION* about the subject.

The **subject of the thesis** relates directly to the topic prompt but expresses the specific area you have chosen to discuss. (Remember the exam topic will be general and will allow you to choose a particular subject related to the topic). For example, the computer is one modern invention.

The **assertion of the thesis** is your viewpoint, or opinion, about the subject. The assertion provides the motive or purpose for your essay, and it may be an arguable point or one that explains or illustrates a point of view.

For example, you may present an argument for or against a particular issue. You may contrast two people, objects, or methods to show that one is better than the other is. You may analyze a situation in all aspects and make recommendations for improvement. You may assert that a law or policy should be adopted, changed, or abandoned. You also, as in the computer example, may explain to your reader that a situation or condition exists; rather than argue a viewpoint, you would use examples to illustrate your assertion about the essay's subject.

Specifically, the **subject** of Topic A is *the computer*. The **assertion** is that *it is a modern wonder that has improved our lives and that we rely on*. Now you quickly have created a workable thesis in a few moments:

> *The computer is a modern wonder of the world that has improved our lives and that we have come to rely on.*

Guidelines for Writing Thesis Statements

The following guidelines are not a formula for writing thesis statements but rather are general strategies for making your thesis statement clearer and more effective.

1.   State a *particular point* of *view* about the topic with both a *subject* and an *assertion*. The thesis should give the essay purpose and scope and thus provide the reader a guide. If the thesis is vague, your essay may be undeveloped because you do not have an idea to assert or a point to explain. Weak thesis statements are often framed as facts, questions, or announcements:

     a.   Avoid a fact statement as a thesis. While a fact statement may provide a subject, it generally does not include a point of view about the subject that provides the basis for an extended discussion. Example: *Recycling saved our community over $10,000 last year.* This fact statement provides a detail, *not* a point of view. Such a detail might be found within an essay but it does not state a point of view.

b.   Avoid framing the thesis as a vague question. In many cases, rhetorical questions do not provide a clear point of view for an extended essay. Example: *How do people recycle?* This question neither asserts a point of view nor helpfully guides the reader to understand the essay's purpose and scope.

c.   Avoid the "announcer" topic sentence that merely states the topic you will discuss.

Example: I *will discuss ways to recycle.* This sentence states the subject but the scope of the essay is only suggested. Again, this statement does not assert a viewpoint that guides the essay's purpose. It merely *announces* that the writer will write about the topic.

2.   Start with a workable thesis. You might revise your thesis as you begin writing and discover your own point of view.

3.   If feasible and appropriate, perhaps state the thesis in multi-point form, expressing the scope of the essay. By stating the points in parallel form, you clearly lay out the essay's plan for the reader.

Example: *To improve the environment, we can recycle our trash, elect politicians who see the environment as a priority, and support lobbying groups who work for environmental protection.*

4.   Because of the exam time limit, place your thesis in the first paragraph to key the reader to the essay's main idea.

Creating a working outline

A good thesis gives structure to your essay and helps focus your thoughts. When forming your thesis, look at your prewriting strategy—clustering, questioning, or brainstorming. Then decide quickly which two or three major areas you will discuss. Remember you must limit *the scope* of the paper because of the time factor.

The **outline** lists those main areas or points as topics for each paragraph. Looking at the prewriting cluster on computers, you might choose several areas in which computers help us, for example, in science and medicine, business, and education. You might also consider people's reliance on this *wonder* and include at least one paragraph about this reliance. A formal outline for this essay might look like the one below.

I.   Introduction and thesis
II. Computers used in science and medicine
II. Computers used in business

IV. Computers used in education
V. People's reliance on computers
VI. Conclusion

Under time pressure, however, you may use a shorter organizational plan, such as abbreviated key words in a list. For example:

1. intro: wonders of the computer OR	a. intro: wonders of computers—science
2. science	b. in the space industry
3. med	c. in medical technology
4. schools	d. conclusion
5. business	
6. conclusion	

Developing the essay

With a working thesis and outline, you can begin writing the essay. The essay should be in three main sections:

1) The **introduction** sets up the essay and leads to the thesis statement.
2) The **body paragraphs** are developed with concrete information leading from the **topic sentences**.
3) The **conclusion** ties the essay together.

Introduction

Put your thesis statement into a clear, coherent opening paragraph. One effective device is to use a funnel approach in which you begin with a brief description of the broader issue and then move to a clearly focused, specific thesis statement.

Consider the following introductions to the essay on computers. The length of each is an obvious difference. Read each and consider the other differences.

Does each introduce the subject generally?
Does each lead to a stated thesis?
Does each relate to the topic prompt?

Introduction 1: *Computers are used every day. They have many uses. Some people who use them are workers, teachers, and doctors.*

Analysis: This introduction does give the general topic, computers used every day, but it does not explain what those uses are. This introduction does not offer a point of view in a clearly stated thesis nor does it convey the idea that computers are a modem wonder.

Introduction 2: *Computers are used just about everywhere these days. I do not think there is an office around that does not use computers, and we use them a lot in all kinds of jobs. Computers are great for making life easier and work better. I do not think we could get along without the computer.*

Analysis: This introduction gives the general topic about computers and mentions one area that uses computers. The thesis states that people could not get along without computers, but it does not state the specific areas the essay discusses. Note, too, the meaning is not helped by vague diction such as *a lot* or *great.*

Introduction 3: *Each day, we either use computers or see them being used around us. We wake to the sound of a digital alarm operated by a microchip. Our cars run by computerized machinery. We use computers to help us learn. We receive phone calls and letters transferred from computers across continents. Our astronauts walked on the moon and returned safely, all because of computer technology. The computer is a wonderful electronic brain that we have come to rely on, and it has changed our world through advances in science, business, and education.*

Analysis: This introduction is the most thorough and fluent because it provides interest in the general topic and offers specific information about computers as a modern wonder. It also leads to a thesis that directs the reader to the scope of the discussion—advances in science, business, and education.

Topic Sentences

Just as the essay must have an overall focus reflected in the thesis statement, each paragraph must have a central idea reflected in the topic sentence. A good topic sentence also provides transition from the previous paragraph and relates to the essay's thesis. Good topic sentences, therefore, provide unity throughout the essay.

Consider the following potential topic sentences. Be sure that each provides transition and clearly states the subject of the paragraph.

Topic Sentence 1: *Computers are used in science.*

Analysis: This sentence simply states the topic—computers used in science. It does not relate to the thesis or provide transition from the introduction. The reader still does not know how computers are used.

Topic Sentence 2: *Now I will talk about computers used in science.*

Analysis: Like the faulty "announcer" thesis statement, this "announcer" topic sentence is vague and merely names the topic.

Topic Sentence 3: *First, computers used in science have improved our lives.*

Analysis: The transition word *First* helps link the introduction and this paragraph. It adds unity to the essay. It, however, does not give specifics about the improvements computers have made in our lives.

Topic Sentence 4: *First used in scientific research and spaceflights, computers are now used extensively in the diagnosis and treatment of disease.*

Analysis: This sentence is the most thorough and fluent. It provides specific areas that will be discussed in the paragraph and it offers more than an announcement of the topic. The writer gives concrete information about the content of the paragraph that will follow.

Summary Guidelines for Writing Topic Sentences
1. Specifically relate the topic to the thesis statement.
2. State clearly and concretely the subject of the paragraph.
3. Provide some transition from the previous paragraph.
4. Avoid topic sentences that are facts, questions, or announcers.

Supporting Details

If you have a good thesis and a good outline, you should be able to construct a complete essay. Your paragraphs should contain concrete, interesting information and supporting details to support your point of view. As often as possible, create images in your reader's mind. Fact statements also add weight to your opinions, especially when you are trying to convince the reader of your viewpoint. Because every good thesis has an assertion, you should offer specifics, facts, data, anecdotes, expert opinion, and other details to *show* or *prove* that assertion. While *you* know what you mean, your *reader* does not. On the exam, you must explain and develop ideas as fully as possible in the time allowed.

In the following paragraph, the sentences in **bold print** provide a skeleton of a paragraph on the benefits of recycling. The sentences in bold are generalizations that, by themselves, do not explain the need to recycle. The sentences in *italics* add details to SHOW the general points in bold. Notice how the supporting details help you understand the necessity for recycling.

While one day recycling may become mandatory in all states, right now, it is voluntary in many communities. *Those of us who participate in recycling are amazed by how much material is recycled.* **For many communities, the blue-box recycling program has had an immediate effect.** *By just recycling glass, aluminum cans, and plastic bottles, we have reduced the volume of disposable trash by one-third, thus extending the useful life of local landfills by over a decade. Imagine the difference if those dramatic results were achieved nationwide.* **The amount of reusable items we thoughtlessly dispose of is staggering.** *For example, Americans dispose of enough steel every day to supply Detroit car manufacturers for three months. Additionally, we dispose of enough aluminum annually to rebuild the nation's air fleet. These statistics, available from the Environmental Protection Agency (EPA), should encourage all of us to watch what we throw away.* **Clearly, recycling in our homes and in our communities directly improves the environment.**

Notice how the author's supporting examples enhance the message of the paragraph and relate to the author's thesis noted above. If you only read the boldface sentences, you have a glimpse at the topic. This paragraph of illustration, however, is developed through numerous details creating specific images: *reduced the volume of disposable trash by one-third; extended the useful life of local landfills by over a decade; enough steel every day to supply Detroit car manufacturers for three months; enough aluminum to rebuild the nation's air fleet.* If the writer had merely written a few general sentences, as those shown in boldface, you would not fully understand the vast amount of trash involved in recycling or the positive results of current recycling efforts.

End your essay with a brief straightforward **concluding paragraph** that ties together the essay's content and leaves the reader with a sense of its completion. The conclusion should reinforce the main points and offer some insight into the topic, provide a sense of unity for the essay by relating it to the thesis, and signal clear closure of the essay.

On the next page is a sample strong response to the prompt:

A problem people recognize and should do something about

Sample Strong Response

Does the introduction help orient the reader to the topic?

Is there a thesis? Does it clearly state the main idea of the essay?

Does each paragraph have a topic sentence that provides transition and defines the idea?

Do the paragraphs purposefully support the thesis? Do they have interesting details and examples?

Time magazine, which typically selects a person of the year, chose Earth as the planet of the year in 1988 to underscore the severe problems facing our planet and therefore us. We hear dismal reports everyday about the water shortage, the ozone depletion, and the obscene volume of trash generated by our society. Because the problem is global, many people feel powerless to help. Fortunately, by being environmentally aware, we can take steps to alter what seems inevitable. We can recycle our trash and support politicians and lobbying groups who will work for laws to protect the environment.

While one day, recycling may be mandatory in all states, right now it is voluntary in many communities. Those of us who participate in recycling are amazed by how much material is recycled. For many communities, the blue-box recycling program has had an immediate effect. By just recycling glass, aluminum cans, and plastic bottles, we have reduced the volume of disposable trash by one-third, thus extending the useful life of local landfills by over a decade. Imagine the difference if those dramatic results were achieved nationwide. The amount of reusable items we thoughtlessly dispose of is staggering. For example, Americans dispose of enough steel every day to supply Detroit car manufacturers for three months. Additionally, we dispose of enough aluminum annually to rebuild the nation's air fleet. These statistics, available from the Environmental Protection Agency (EPA) should encourage us to watch what we throw away. Clearly, recycling in our homes and communities directly improves the environment.

Are the paragraphs unified and coherent? Is the material in each paragraph relevant and important?

Moreover, we must be aware of the political issues involved in environmental protection because, unfortunately, the environmental crisis continues despite policies and laws on the books. Enacted in the 1970s, the federal Clean Water Act was intended to clean up polluted waters throughout the nation and to provide safe drinking water for everyone. However, today, with the Water Act still in place, dangerous medical waste has washed onto public beaches in Florida and recently several people died from the polluted drinking water in Madison, Wisconsin. Additionally, contradictory government policies often work against resource protection. For example, some state welfare agencies give new mothers money only for disposable, not cloth, diapers. In fact, consumer groups found that cloth diapers are cheaper initially and save money over time as we struggle with the crisis of bulging landfills. Clearly, we need consistent government policies and stiffer laws to ensure mandatory enforcement and heavy fines for polluters. We can do this best by electing politicians who will fight for such laws and voting out those who will not.

Does the conclusion tie the essay together?

We can also work to save our planet by supporting organizations that lobby for meaningful, enforceable legal changes. Most of us do not have time to write letters, send telegrams, or study every issue concerning the environment. We can join several organizations that act as watchdogs for us all. For example, organizations such as Greenpeace, the Cousteau Society, and the Sierra Club all offer memberships for as low as 15 dollars. By supporting these organizations, we ensure that they have the necessary resources to keep working for all of us and do not have to alter their standards because they must accept funding from special interest groups.

Is the essay edited for grammar and mechanical errors?

Clearly, we all must become environmentally aware. Only through increased awareness, can we avoid the tragic consequences of living on a dying planet. We must actively support recycling programs and support those who fight to protect our fragile environment.

Analysis: While not every essay needs to be this thorough in order to pass the exam, this essay shows that with a clear thesis and concept in mind, a writer can produce a literate, interesting piece at one sitting. The introduction creates interest in the general topic and leads to a thesis in the last sentence. The reader has a very clear idea of what will be addressed in the essay, and all body paragraphs have topic sentences that relate to the thesis and provide transition. The numerous supporting details and examples are presented in a sophisticated style that reads easily and is enhanced by a college-level vocabulary and word choice. Transition words and phrases add unity to sentences and paragraphs. Grammar and mechanics areas are correct, so errors do not detract from the fine writing. For all these reasons, this essay is a polished piece of writing deserving of an upper-range score.

XAMonline, INC. 21 Orient Ave. Melrose, MA 02176
Toll Free number 800-509-4128
TO ORDER Fax 781-662-9268 OR www.XAMonline.com
GEORGIA ASSESSMENTS FOR THE CERTIFICATION OF EDUCATORS -GACE - 2008

PO#   Store/School:

Address 1:

Address 2 (Ship to other):

City, State Zip

Credit card number_____-_____-_____-_____   **expiration**_____
EMAIL _____
PHONE   **FAX**

13# ISBN 2007	TITLE	Qty	Retail	Total
978-1-58197-257-3	Basic Skills 200, 201, 202			
978-1-58197-528-4	Biology 026, 027			
978-1-58197-529-1	Science 024, 025			
978-1-58197-341-9	English 020, 021			
978-1-58197-569-7	Physics 030, 031			
978-1-58197-531-4	Art Education Sample Test 109, 110			
978-1-58197-545-1	History 034, 035			
978-1-58197-527-7	Health and Physical Education 115, 116			
978-1-58197-540-6	Chemistry 028, 029			
978-1-58197-534-5	Reading 117, 118			
978-1-58197-547-5	Media Specialist 101, 102			
978-1-58197-535-2	Middle Grades Reading 012			
978-1-58197-539-0	Middle Grades Science 014			
978-1-58197-345-7	Middle Grades Mathematics 013			
978-1-58197-546-8	Middle Grades Social Science 015			
978-158-197-573-4	Middle Grades Language Arts 011			
978-1-58197-346-4	Mathematics 022, 023			
978-1-58197-549-9	Political Science 032, 033			
978-1-58197-544-4	Paraprofessional Assessment 177			
978-1-58197-542-0	Professional Pedagogy Assessment 171, 172			
978-1-58197-259-7	Early Childhood Education 001, 002			
978-1-58197-548-2	School Counseling 103, 104			
978-1-58197-541-3	Spanish 141, 142			
978-1-58197-610-6	Special Education General Curriculum 081, 082			
978-1-58197-530-7	French Sample Test 143, 144			
			SUBTOTAL	
	FOR PRODUCT PRICES GO TO WWW.XAMONLINE.COM		Ship	$8.25
			TOTAL	

Printed in the United States
123429LV00001B/95-102/P